Judi James is a leading television behaviour, image, workplace cu and has her own Channel Five series, *Naked Celebrity*. Judi also appears regularly on *Big Brother*, *The Xtra Factor*, *Newsnight* and *Sky News*.

Judi started her career as a leading catwalk model and trained many big names at her modelling school in Chelsea, including Naomi Campbell. She has had six novels published, including the bestseller *Supermodel*, and has written eight non-fiction books. Judi also writes regular weekly columns for *You* magazine and has a celebrity problem page in *Zest*.

'We need someone like Judi to slash through the spin and show us what the stars really mean' *Daily Mail*

'Top image consultant and body language guru' *Elle*

'Body language ace' *Cosmo Girl*

POKER FACE

How to win poker at the table and online

Judi James

LONDON

1 3 5 7 9 10 8 6 4 2

Published in 2007 by Vermilion, an imprint of Ebury Publishing

Ebury Publishing is a division of the Random House Group

The Random House Group Limited Reg. No. 954009

Addresses for companies within the Random House Group can be found at
www.randomhouse.co.uk

A CIP catalogue record is available for this book from the British Library.

The Random House Group Limited makes every effort to ensure that the
papers used in our books are made from trees that have been legally sourced
from well-managed and credibly certified forests. Our paper procurement
policy can be found on
www.randomhouse.co.uk

Printed and bound in Great Britain by
Cox & Wyman Ltd, Reading, Berkshire

ISBN: 9780091912918

CONTENTS

INTRODUCTION

Poker is one of the greatest games of simple psychology ever invented. In many ways it's all about lying. Whereas other card games are largely one-dimensional, with tension and success reliant on a combination of chance and skills of focus and memory, poker throws another vital and dramatic dimension into the pot.

Winning at poker is like winning at life. To play well you need more than a lucky hand. That exciting extra dimension is all about people skills: having the ability to read your opponents' body language and block their attempts to read yours. All of this can be subconscious. You might not even know you're assimilating all these subtle complex signals. But by reading this book you're going to find out how to make it a conscious process. Then, instead of getting a 'feeling' about another player and whether they're bluffing or not, you'll be able to work analytically to cut down the chances of making a mistake by random assessments.

Poker skill can be neatly divided into two categories: play skill and psychological skill. The game itself might be simple but the psychology of bluffing and unmasking the bluffs is satisfyingly complex. This book is going to explain all about the body language skills necessary to play poker and win. And, as a bonus, you'll be learning how to read other people in life in general. Unmasking a liar isn't just reserved for the poker table!

WHO NEEDS TO READ IT?

I make no assumptions about your poker skills or experience. This book is aimed at new players, professional players and all those in between. You could play for peanuts or Smarties with your Aunty and Uncle, or you could be chomping cheroots and playing for zillions in some dimly lit gambling den for all I care. You might not even have started to play poker yet, in which case I'd suggest you give the gambling den a wide berth, at least until you've learnt the basics. This book will also be extremely useful for people who have absolutely no interest in poker (although it will have been an odd choice of purchase as it has the word 'Poker' in the title).

IF IT'S THAT EASY WHY DON'T YOU CLEAN UP AT POKER?

The first question everyone asks a clairvoyant or psychic is: Can you predict the winner of the Grand National? I'm not sure what the stock answer is but it is generally along the lines of 'not wanting to use my talent for personal gain'. So what I *could* say is that it wouldn't be ethical to employ my unique powers as a body language expert at the poker table as it would give me an unfair advantage. But of course, that would be rubbish.

For one thing, I'm not that virtuous. If body language were a precise science and if I were a better actor and if I had nerves of steel and a ruthless streak you'd find me in Las Vegas cleaning up.

But I'm not. So here's the deal: I have been studying and writing about body language for over 20 years. Most of my work is done in the world of business. A year ago I was asked to give body language tips on a DVD about poker. And suddenly I discovered a whole new outlet for body language skills. It was a little like Stephen Hawking discovering his theory of 'space time' could be used to win at Monopoly.

I decided to start by seeing what's already around in terms of advice. One thing I discovered was that most of the great Bibles of poker currently on the market are (a) American and (b) too technical for people with a short attention-span.

Tips on poker body language tend to come from experienced poker players who learnt their psychological skills around the poker table. They look from the inside out. This is fine, but I needed to explore from the opposite direction. I'm looking from the outside in. I'm a body language expert who is applying her knowledge here to one specific use.

GEEK IS THE NEW POKER CHIC

What I also considered is the new breed of poker players that are flooding the market:

- Office workers – who already know a lot about body language because they sit in meetings all day trying to look as though they know what they're talking about.
- Younger people – who don't want to wear Stetsons and eye shades and sit counting the beads of sweat on their opponents' faces or watching exactly how they crumble their Oreo cookies when they're placing a bet.

The link between business skills and poker skills is obvious and it's probably why poker has become the pastime of choice for so many young professionals. What you hone at work you use around the poker table and what you learn around the poker table you use to improve your performance at work.

If you want to be Paul Newman or Clint Eastwood then this book isn't for you. If you want to take some of your business skills of bluffing, influencing and unmasking and apply them to the art of winning at poker then it is 'the real deal'.

ONLINE POKER

I have included a chapter about the psychology of playing poker on the Internet. Online poker is one of the fastest-growing games in the UK. And both Internet and celebrity games are fuelling a passion for poker and creating a newer, younger generation of players who cut their teeth online but then progress to the real thing as their confidence and interest grows. For example, Chris Moneymaker won the World Series of Poker having begun his playing career only a few years before, gambling on the Internet. He had been inspired by watching the Matt Damon film *Rounders*.

It could seem on the surface that online play makes the need for poker faces and visual bluffs redundant, in the same way that telephones and e-mails impacted on our conversations by appearing to remove the need for body language. And yet body language and non-verbal communication will always survive any form of electronic communication you care to throw at it. Honestly.

How do I know? Well, I bet you still use your hands when you're speaking on the phone. And that's not just some simian-throwback-style trait. However anonymous we make our communications, the recipients will always crave to dig deeper and get to the truth. Don't tell me you never pondered over a very simple e-mail message wondering what the sender *really* meant? We still like to pick up on smaller details to give clues about the person 'talking'.

On the phone we listen to the changes in the timbre of the voice and the subtle rhythms of breathing and speech to tell if someone's stressed or hiding the truth. Online players tend to swear by odds and logic but there's still scope for psychology. They're tuned in to the length of pauses before play and the chat-box messages. Even the names that players adopt are used to glean clues about them.

HOW TO USE THIS BOOK

This book is written in two parts. Part One focuses on you. Self-knowledge and self-examination are fascinating and critical. During this section we'll study everything to do with bluffing, lying and your poker 'performance', including understanding your own motivations and approach to the game, which will in turn have a crucial impact on your performance success. Part Two will place your opponents under the microscope. We'll see how they bluff and why they bluff and how to spot clues that will reveal what they're really thinking or planning. To start, in Chapters 1 and 2, I lay out the background to everything you're about to learn.

PART ONE: ALL ABOUT YOU

1

POKER AND PSYCHOLOGY

Psychology – I hate that word. By sticking an -ology onto virtually anything we make it sound precious and inaccessible to anyone who doesn't wear a beard and sandals with socks. Try it yourself:

Shop*ology*
Bath*ology*
Smile*ology*
Bingedrinking*ology*

Psychology is the study of human behaviour. Now, call me an intellectual minimalist if you like, but I'd assume you've already done quite a lot of that in your life. So this is one -ology that is accessible to everyone, all the time, without the need for sandals and socks. Psychology is all about us being us. What drives us and what creates our behaviour. This is one science that we all had a head start in whether we excelled at school or not. The one difference with psychology is that, instead of just watching how the human animal performs, it goes one step further and asks: 'Why?'

And here's the problem for most of us. Not only did your parents drum into you that 'It's rude to stare', thus hindering your ability to read other humans accurately, they were also struggling to quash your constant and unrelenting use of that word 'Why?' It drove them mad, like fingernails on a chalkboard. 'Why? Why? Why? Why? Why? Why?' This one comment might have dashed your hopes of being a top poker player, winning squillions in Vegas. That's because to be a really good player you need to be good at human behaviour and the 'Why' that lies behind what we all do.

RORKE'S DRIFT

Remember that scene in the film *Zulu*, when the Brits are about to get annihilated in yet another attack and one young soldier asks his sergeant: 'Why us Sarge?' Instead of a discourse on fate and chance and the realities of life he gets a parental-style response: 'Because we're here, laddie, because we're here.' That sergeant would never have made a good psychologist. Psychologists were the kids who never stopped asking: 'Why?' This means that instead of being voyeurs of human behaviour we can also begin to predict it. By working out what drives and motivates it we can begin to spot patterns. Not magical, non-negotiable patterns that are set in concrete or carved onto rock like the Ten Commandments but likely patterns and useful patterns.

Here's an example of how psychology can be applied to everyday life: You know how it is when you walk up to the double doors leading into a department store and the door you choose to push open is invariably the one that's still locked? How annoying is that? Now, if it was your store you could apply a little psychology to the problem and make it go away. There is a pattern to our door choices. In general we all tend to go for the same door. Even an armchair psychologist could work out which door should be the one to open to cause less hassle to customers.

We're going to apply the same brilliance to your game of poker. Not everyone will choose the door on the right and not everyone will use predictable or readable body language when they're playing poker. But a lot will. And it's the ones that do that will help you win and win again.

BODY TALK

First, a brief history of body language. You started to use it to your advantage at the age of about 15 minutes. You've been using it ever since to read and communicate with other people. So you must be pretty good at it by now. The only reason you're not as good as other animals is that by about the age of two years you were being told by a well-meaning parent that it's rude to stare. Nobody said this to your cat or dog, which is why they're much better at judging other cats and dogs. In most face-to-face communication, body language accounts for over half the perceived impact of the message. Okay, I said I'd keep it short. And now the update . . .

TV PUNDITS

We're all experts at body language but it's only recently that this essential form of communication has been consciously rediscovered, thanks in part to the emergence of the reality TV show in our daily cultural life. Suddenly we're able to watch other people without any of them turning to the screen and saying, 'It's rude to stare.' Programmes like *Big Brother* create a 'human zoo' environment so that at last we can observe our own race in captivity and learn all about human behaviours and communication skills. Suddenly it is good to stare. And we do it in our millions.

What we learn from shows like this is how much information the human animal gives away via his/her non-verbal signals. Armchair critics now assess whether contestants are being deceitful or two-faced and can see their mood swings and inner thoughts writ large on their faces and in their gestures.

One of the first things we learn is that screen and stage actors, no matter how good, are rubbish at body language. For centuries they've been feeding us a range of gestures, expressions and prop usage that only exist on screen or stage. Their job has been to point up their thoughts to the audience via the use of various thespian contrivances. We're helped to understand the characters and their thoughts by whopping great visual clues. But real life isn't like that. People on reality TV are trying to mask their inner thoughts, just like most of us do in the workplace. And poker players are not *trying* to be an open book to their audience.

What we look for in reality TV is what we seek in life: a better understanding of the people we're dealing with. We want to read between the lines. Despite the masking that they attempt for the cameras, we can tell when participants in reality shows are annoyed, stressed, upset or irritated – even though they might be in a state of verbal denial for the sake of colony peace. So, when one character asks another, 'Are you all right?' we can read from their slumped posture or eye movements that when their verbal response is 'yeah' they're actually lying, either out of politeness or because they think that verbalising the problem will lead to conflict.

So, your TV viewing choices could already be helping you to improve your poker game. But how much does monitoring someone's body language around the poker table or even in the boardroom help give an insight into the workings of their mind?

MIND-READING AND FORTUNE-TELLING

How great and yet how enormously spooky would it be if we could read each other's minds? Imagine if our internal conversations appeared writ large above our heads in cartoon-style 'thought bubbles' for all to see. Now, imagine that this has suddenly happened. You woke up this morning and those 'thought bubbles' had popped up overnight. When you kissed your partner and said, 'How did you sleep?' your 'thought bubble' added, *'Because I didn't – your snoring kept me awake all night.'* Or when your boss asked whether you could finish off a last-minute proposal and your mouth said, 'No problem', your thought bubble contradicted with, *'although I'd rather shove it where the sun don't shine'.*

Now this is your dilemma. You can read other people's minds but – guess what? They can read yours too! Call me clairvoyant, but I'm guessing your next move would be to try to delete your own 'thought bubbles' although you'd probably be more than happy to continue to read other people's.

READ AND DELETE

One of the core aims of this book is to help you do just that. While you're playing poker your body language behaviour acts rather like one of those 'thought bubbles', telling people how you're feeling and what your intentions are. To play poker and win you'll need to learn how to delete your 'thought bubbles'. In practice this means masking your own signals with your poker face, or putting up a smoke-screen by bluffing and acting the opposite to how you feel.

But you'll also want to have a good old look at your opponents' body language 'thought bubbles' at the same time.

Read, but don't reveal. Now, before you learn how to be a reader of 'thought bubbles' you'll also need to remember one very important fact: *Reading body language is not 100 per cent precise or accurate*.

Reading body language gives a better *insight* into a person's mind. But it's not infallible. In many ways you'll be trying to create structure out of chaos. I wish it *was* precise, accurate and easy but it isn't. But it's better to know that before you start.

I worry when I read books that tell you with great authority that one gesture means this and another means that, a kind of 'Eye-Spy' approach to gestures and expressions. But it doesn't work like that. If it did we'd all be on the stage earning pots of money performing mind-reading acts.

There's complexity involved and there's a degree of randomness. But don't let that put you off. All knowledge is useful as a tool. You just need to know that its success is variable and a lot depends on who's wielding that tool.

DITCH THE 'TELLS'

Another thing you need to know about this book is that we're not going to use the term 'tells'. Sorry. I know they sound thrilling. Now poker 'tells' are famous. If you haven't come across them before – if you are a 'tell' virgin – then rest assured you'll hear the term sooner or later once you start to get into the game of poker.

Put simply, a 'tell' is a body language give-away. It's that small glance or pursing of the lips that is alleged to pass on information to your opponents about the type of hand you are holding. A 'tell' can be conscious – by employing effective acting skills to bluff your opponent – or it can be subconscious – by giving the game away via your habit of cleaning one ear with your toothpick each time you hold a poor hand.

Tells provide dramatic and memorable key cinematic moments. Every book of poker cites the scene in *Rounders* where winning the pot depended on someone spotting a 'tell' that involved the way an Oreo cookie was broken. This story is now touted as though it happened for real, sending millions of US poker players off panning for gold by watching for changes in biscuit-breaking. If you're lucky enough to have an opponent who dunks a Rich Tea just as they're raising a bet then go ahead and gamble accordingly, but body language reading is generally not that simple.

Which is why the term 'tell' is misleading. What it should be is 'hint' or even 'suggest'. Either one of these terms would be more honest but obviously way less sexy than 'tell'. But I do hope you can appreciate that it's better to start from a position of honesty. If I use the 'tell' word about body language gestures in this book you'll go off placing large bets just because someone scratched his nose as he raised and then you'll lose your shirt and blame me.

I know you want the definitive guide to foolproof mind-reading but, despite numerous claims to the contrary, body language is not a precise science. So we're going to use different terms. This is now officially a 'tell-free' zone. We're going to call unconscious, hinting signals 'leakage' and the conscious movements aimed at bluffing 'performance gestures'.

Don't bother arguing, that's just the way it is. I don't want your kids going without shoes because you gambled all your savings on the crumble of a custard cream!

ALL ABOUT LYING

The game of poker is a game for liars.

Simon Freedman has been playing poker for 14 years, mostly with friends and newcomers in their own poker schools. According to Simon, when you play poker:

'You play the player, not the cards. You're trying to assess the other players psychologically and sometimes you're kicking yourself internally, too. Playing poker's about understanding people. It's like driving a racing car. When you know where all the gear knobs are then you can use your skill on top of that.'

John Duthie started playing poker in 1991, having watched some players in his local casino. He sent off for books on poker from the Gamblers bookstore in Las Vegas and taught himself. John was the first winner of the Ladbrokes Poker Million in 2000.

John is equally adamant about the role bluffing and lying has in the game of poker:

'Every experienced player is constantly wary of all other players at the table, because we all know the same tricks and the game develops into a battle of wits rather than luck. As the amount of money played for increases, the more psychological the game becomes. There is a level where only the cards count and

*then there are levels where being aware of your opponents'
abilities is far more significant. For example, if you know a player
is capable of laying down a big hand, then you know that you can
successfully bluff that player and vice versa.'*

Poker players lie in one of two ways:

- *By hiding their true feelings.* This tends to occur
  throughout a game and is what is normally referred to as
  keeping a 'poker face'. This requires stillness and the ability
  to be deadpan. The idea is to delete your 'thought bubbles'
  totally by displaying a blank sheet. You give nothing away
  at all.
- *By acting in the opposite way to their real feelings.* This is
  called 'bluffing'. Instead of playing possum, you actively
  perform. If you have a strong hand you act out a response
  that implies it's a weak one, to keep your opponents from
  folding. If you have a weak hand you pretend it's a strong
  one, to make them fold out of fear.

While a 'poker face' can and often does occur throughout a game,
bluffing will often be used as an occasional weapon of choice.
Devlin Tagoe, a TV researcher who has been playing poker with
friends for just under a year, explains: *'I find poker thrilling. For
me, the possibility of winning money off a friend is a good thing.
One friend refuses to play for money with friends but we all know
what we're getting into. I operate a style of misinformation and
disinformation. For instance, I over-talk each hand if I'm doing
well or if I'm doing badly. I like to ask a lot of questions and lead
them a dance. It's all about creating a fog of confusion.'*

Bluffs need to be varied or you won't fool the other players for long. Your opponents will see you've bluffed as soon as your cards are on the table and will keep it in mind for the next hand. So it's up to you to decide how many times that bluff might work. Then you're into the world of bluff, double-bluff or no bluff at all.

When you play against low-skill players they won't notice whether you bluff or not. They'll be too busy worrying about their own game to spot your performance. But if and when you start to play with more skilled players, you'll need to use deception because they'll be watching and analysing your behaviour patterns for signs of clues and leakage and you'll need to:

- Analyse your own body language to see what they can see and to stem any leaks that do occur and
- Monitor your opponents' behaviour to look for similar patterns or traits.

If you think bluffing is easy you'll have made your first mistake. Listen to John Duthie: *'I have had to learn the skill of bluffing, but I am forever looking for ways to improve my ability. When I bluff I am constantly aware of everything about my body language, breathing and pulse rate. I try to maintain a completely trance-like state, but will also occasionally adopt certain techniques to cover up the trait.'*

For Simon Freedman, a bluff doesn't just include table performance either: *'A bluff can last for a whole evening: what you wear, how you offer drinks, and even something as small as a sigh will all give out information about you. It's all about you as a person, how you can make them misjudge and miscalculate you.'*

Devlin Tagoe is aware of the problems of trying to bluff friends: 'One of my friends can read me no matter what I do but I can always confuse him at poker. My biggest give-away is my eyes. I find it hard not to smile. My mouth starts to turn up and I can feel myself struggling not to smile when I've got that rush of joy and adrenaline that comes from having a good hand. I can normally smile at the slightest thing and I can even feel sweat forming or a cold flush from the effort it takes.'

If you never bluff at all then your opponents will usually fold when you bet high because they'll know you have a better hand. Similarly, they know they'll be able to frighten you out of the game with a big bet. So bluffing is a big part of the game.

However, remember the two great rules of bluffing that are hammered home in nearly every book of poker I have ever read:

1. Only bluff when you have a reasonable chance of succeeding.
2. Only bluff opponents who can be bluffed.

You also have to be consistent in your focus.

With both a poker face and a bluff it will be your job to delve into your opponent's 'thought bubbles'. To do this you'll be studying their body language for give-aways and clues.

SPOTTING THE LIAR OR BEING EXPOSED

When you choose to study poker body language you need to know what you're looking for and why, both in your own signals and those of other players.

There are three key aspects to be aware of in others and in yourself:

1. Whether leakage gestures or actions are giving you/them away.
2. Whether your opponent is employing performed gestures to bluff you.
3. Whether your own performed gestures or actions are working.

You must also be aware of how people act generally – their personality and overall behaviour trends. And, of course, this applies to you too. Let's look at these key aspects in more detail.

LEAKAGE

In face-to-face communication, the greatest impact of the message comes from the way the words are said and the body language that goes with them, rather than the words themselves. The impact of a perceived message breaks down like this:

- *Words*: As little as 7 per cent impact. We distrust words and have a limited memory for who said what.
- *Vocal tone*: Around 38 per cent impact. It gives emphasis and meaning to your words.
- *Non-verbal*: As much as 55 per cent impact. We remember the visual signals longer and tend to judge them as being more honest.

Congruence and incongruence

When you speak to other people and you actually mean what you say, your communication will usually be 'congruent'. This means your words, your vocal tone and your non-verbal communications will all appear to be in harmony. However, when you lie it is difficult to keep your verbal and non-verbal communications emotionally synchronised. Your communication is 'incongruent'.

You can often spot small signals that appear to be 'leaking' the truth. Leakage usually involves those parts of the body that are less easy to control, or less thought about, such as hands and feet. We'll be discussing and analysing all the 'leakage' possibilities from breathing to eye movement to blinking later on.

In poker you should look for leakage at any time from any player. But it will be particularly useful if your opponent has attempted to close down his or her body language in a poker face. If they've decided static is the best technique then you'll need to study their leakage to gain useful insights.

PERFORMED GESTURES

These are the poker bluffs. If players decide to act out their responses and emotions in a bid to confuse or mislead they'll employ performed gestures. Whereas the poker face requires stillness and a closing down of natural responses, performed gestures are more complex. They involve suppressing your natural responses but then acting the exact opposite.

So if you have a good hand you'll need to hide your excitement and feign boredom or lack of interest. If you have a bad one you'll strive to keep the disappointment or frustration hidden from view and create a mask of anticipation or excitement instead. This type of body language performance involves two stages instead of just one in the case of the poker face.

READING PEOPLE

Once you learn to read people you'll gain an insight into their general behaviour patterns rather than a single quirk. By being ultra-perceptive about your opponents you will increase your chances of winning by second-guessing their style of play. And by understanding human nature you can begin to assess each type of player and predict the types of decisions they'll make during a game. Are they high-risk or safe players? Do they think analytically or will they tend to work on impulse and emotion? Are they likely to bluff or will they play in a straightforward manner?

When should I be analysing body language?

Any and all parts of a game are good times to study other players. Never think that you should only be perceptive while you're in the game. You should start looking the moment your opponents arrive and continue to watch them play even while you're out of the game. Look for patterns, personalities and habits. If you learn your opponents' behaviour patterns you'll recognise when they break them.

READING YOURSELF

Of course, the most important person you need to analyse is yourself. How do you respond to winning or losing? What motivates you to play? Why do you want to beat your opponents?

Are you genuinely ruthless enough to lie to other players or will it trip your 'guilt switch' or trigger your basic desire to be liked?

The pain of awareness when you're learning

You should be aware of your own body language at all times. The more often you examine it the better, and I'll tell you why: thinking consciously about your own body language makes you uncomfortable. This discomfort creates awkwardness. It's very much a part of the learning process and the sooner you go through the 'pain' barrier the better. These are the four stages of learning:

- *Unconscious error*: Your normal body language is certain to be full of mistakes, leaking away too much information to your opponents via gestures, postures and facial movements. However, your state of unawareness is well within your comfort zone. 'What I don't know can't hurt me' will be your thinking. How wrong can you be? Other players are happily cleaning up because your eye movements are giving away the state of your hand.

- *Conscious error*: At last someone points out that you cough, sniff or scratch when you get worried. You move directly into the 'zone of acute discomfort'. Now you're feeling paranoid about every movement you make and your body language no longer looks natural. When you try to move you resemble a *Thunderbirds* puppet. You wish you'd never been told about your body language. Now it's even worse and you toy with the idea of ignoring it. After all, you weren't losing every game before.

- *Conscious improvement*: If you stick with it (and I'm hoping you will) your body language will improve. You'll still be well within the discomfort zone but – like driving a car – it gets more comfortable the more you do it.

- *Unconscious improvement*: This is the good stage. It hasn't been easy but your new, improved body language can now be employed while you're within your comfort zone. The integration is complete and you don't even know you're doing it.

POKER PERFORMERS, FROM DOWNPLAYERS TO DIVAS

Poker 'performances' vary according to a player's preference or level of experience. I've grouped them into four key categories but keep in mind that people don't stick to one throughout their poker-playing lives. There's natural movement as experience grows and so you need to avoid stereotyping and keep looking for change.

Downplayers

These are most likely to be inexperienced players. They're so absorbed with learning the basics that they're too busy to give an Oscar-winning performance. They're also unlikely to alter their betting decisions because of subtle theatrical touches from you. They're probably too wrapped up in their own thoughts to notice if you blow your nose or give a burst on the banjo. They could be more experienced players who have a compulsion to honesty at all times. Or maybe they just don't see the point of muddying the purity of the game by adding a little psychological drama, in which case they should move on to a less challenging game, like Snap or Happy Families.

POKER FACE

Walk-ons and bit-part players

These are the more experienced players who are just getting into the knockabout fun that comes from bluffing at poker. They've played enough to know how it's done and they're keen to flex their thespian muscles. These bluffers tend to be erratic and often lack any pattern or habit to pick up on, which can make them a bigger risk than you might think. They notice very little as their own performances excite them to the point that they're not receiving 'incoming mail'. As they gain experience they'll start to notice your signals, either on a conscious or subconscious level, but they're still relatively easy to scam.

Key players

These are poker's 'higher performers'. They're skilled players who prepare well before they perform and perceive. As well as boasting lots of experience, they usually have preferred techniques and tricks. They enjoy bluffing and although they're always tempted by the opportunity to flaunt their performance style they also have the discipline to employ a poker face now and again.

Poker divas

These are the seasoned, experienced pros who at one time would have had a red ring around their head from the Stetson they'd been wearing or would have been sporting an eye-shade. They'll bluff, double-bluff and possibly triple-bluff and they assume their opponents will do the same. Their mastery of the poker face is so absolute that they refuse to remove it even when away from the table.

They're method actors, with the same level of role preparation to the game that the likes of Daniel Day Lewis and Al Pacino bring to a movie role. They act like Clint Eastwood in *Dirty Harry* most of the time, whether playing at the tables or romping with the kids at home. These are people who live and breathe the game of poker. They may even have suppressed their natural bodily functions and responses to the point where they could give David Blaine a good run for his money.

But don't let all this put you off. You don't need to be capable of bowel and breathing mastery to enjoy poker. In fact, you'll very likely have more fun if you don't. And – as you know – I'd be happier if we kept this book a Stetson-free zone.

I know there are players in the top US tournaments who enjoy sporting all the old *Showboat/Dallas* gear but we're going to be a bit less camp. Don't forget, I'm writing for a new generation of poker players who've probably started online. And if you've ever sat staring at the screen clad in eye-shades or a cowboy hat with a ring on every finger then move away from the table now!

PLAYING THE GAME

To explain the context in which body language will be helpful, it is useful to look at the three main types of poker being played today: draw poker, Texas hold'em and five-card stud. Specific details vary, but these are the general points.

Draw poker

Draw poker features in classic Westerns and gangster movies. It's a bluffer's paradise! You're dealt five 'hole' or 'pocket' cards face down. Players can only see their own cards – no-one else's. After a round of betting, based on that initial hand, you can replace ('draw') some or all of your cards if you wish, or stick to what you have. This is followed by more betting. You can match the bet ('call'), increase the bet ('raise'), or throw your hand in ('fold'). Initially, you may even be allowed to skip a bet ('check').

As you don't know your opponents' cards, and they don't know yours, you must bluff your heart out. And you bluff in the way you bet. For example, if you have a good hand you might bet low to bluff others into staying in the game so that the winnings (pot) will grow. If your hand is marginal you might bet high to bluff others into folding. Either way, your opponents are expecting you to bluff, and will do the same. So you (and they) must vary the betting pattern to keep everyone guessing. This makes mastering body language vital, to tell if your opponents' betting pattern is a true reflection of their hand, and to hide the strength or weakness of your own.

Texas hold'em

This one dominates TV poker shows, tournaments and online games. Initially, players get two face-down ('pocket' or 'hole') cards, followed by a round of betting. If two or more players stay in, three community cards ('the flop') are dealt face up for all to use. This is followed by another betting round. If two or more players are left, a fourth community card ('the turn') is dealt, face up, followed by more betting. Finally a fifth community card ('the river') is dealt, and there's more betting. Players make the best five-card hand they can using their two 'hole' cards and any three of the community cards.

Five-card stud

In five-card stud, players are dealt two cards initially: one face down and one face up. Then players bet or fold. If two or more players stay in they get a third face-up card, followed by more betting. This continues until, finally, any players left in get a fifth face-up card, followed by more betting. The aim is to make your best hand with the cards you have at each stage, up to a total of five cards. (Seven-card stud is like it, but players get three cards initially and the final (seventh) card is dealt face down.)

Texas hold'em and stud poker differ from draw poker in that a player's fortunes may change with each new card. Plus some cards are visible. This makes it harder to read your opponents' body language (a bonus for them) and harder for them to mask their body language and read yours (a bonus for you).

The hands

Body language expertise is no substitute for poker skill. You must learn which hands to play, in which position, and which ones to fold, as well as the possible hands your opponents can make. You must also remember which visible cards, if any, have folded. This all needs practice.

Playing the player

Good poker is like angling: knowing when to draw your opponents in and when to 'strike' and win the pot. For example, if you have strong 'hole' cards you can decide whether to play for an early win or let the pot build and take a risk that your opponent's hand may improve as more cards are dealt. Your ability to 'play the player' in this way becomes much easier once you learn how to read your opponents' body language – and master your own.

So – if you've got rid of that cheroot let's get on with the process of learning how to use body language to win at poker!

3

YOUR POKER PERFORMANCE IN THE MAKING

I don't ask you to delve deep but I do ask you to delve.

This chapter is dedicated to the mechanics and psychology of your behaviour around the poker table as you prepare to do combat with your opponents. It is essential that you study this information because in order to play well you must first understand the physiological processes involved in your thinking and decisions and how that impacts on your body language.

Look at the 'triangle of improved behaviour' overleaf and consider the impact your inner thoughts have on feelings and behaviour. The dialogues in your head send messages to your subconscious which, in turn, will begin to formulate feelings and emotions. Then there's the link between those feelings and your behaviour. Nearly everything we do is linked to our emotional motivations. But see how that behaviour will, in turn, impact on your thoughts. The Think–Feel–Behave link is continuous. Each one impacts on the other unless you do something to break the pattern.

Triangle of improved behaviour

Negative thinking leads to a downward spiral. For example, if you have negative thoughts about your hand it can cause an attack of nerves. This will lead to anxious behaviour and body language signals, which can affect the way you play the situation. This can, in turn, convince you that you were right to have those negative thoughts in the first place. You are then even more likely to view your situation negatively the next time. This reverse affirmation process will produce consistently bad results.

How does this work in practice? Imagine you're new to the game and playing an experienced opponent. You think to yourself, 'He's better than me.' This causes feelings of nervousness or anxiety. These feelings, in turn, trigger anxious body language, such as sweating, and self-comfort gestures like fiddling or tapping, or even shallow breathing. And this behaviour will impact on your thoughts. Once your opponent has cleaned up you'll say to yourself, 'I knew that was going to happen. I should never have played such a good player.' This will guarantee you lose against him next time, too.

So now we're going to look at ways to break the chain. You can do that at any one of the three key points. If you change your thinking you change your feelings. Work on your feelings, like stress or lack of confidence, and your body language improves automatically. Or make changes to your body language, your external signals, and they'll affect your internal messages, making you feel as good as you look.

In Chapter 5 we'll be working on your inner thoughts and your feelings. This section is vital for your poker playing as you'll be performing the 'extended lie'. The longer you lie the more pressure you're put under. This pressure will impact on your body language, making the chances of 'leakage' even greater as the truth about your real feelings and thoughts starts to emerge.

But first you need to get to know yourself a little better. Remember, psychology is all about the 'why'. And your first step is to keep in mind that we're all just animals. A brief look at the behaviour of the human animal and his closest relatives will give a fascinating insight into your behaviour at the poker table.

KNOW YOURSELF!

Self-knowledge is vital for a good poker performance. We all need sound 'intrapersonal skills' – that is, an ability to know what we're like and why we do what we do. Otherwise behaviour is random. Now . . . don't get me wrong. I love spontaneity. People who lack it are anal and sad. But spontaneity has its place. What's great in the bedroom is rubbish at the card table.

Winning at poker is all about first understanding and then suppressing your instinctive urges and thinking. Great poker is about harnessing that aggressive energy so that it works for you rather than against.

SIMIAN SIMILARITIES

Let's start by examining the roots of your body language behaviours. By understanding the source you'll find it easier to analyse and define current poker body language signals and what they really mean when they're used.

How well do you understand your own behaviour and what prompts it? Possibly not very well at all. Often it's not until we're put under pressure to 'perform' at the poker table, job interview or business presentation that we begin to be self-analytical. By that stage all we're concerned about is dealing with and suppressing the visual symptoms of negative emotions like nerves, anxiety or fear. But to deal with those symptoms effectively you need to understand what's happening and why.

THE AGGRESSIVE APE

In his book on human behaviour where he compared us to our nearest relatives, Desmond Morris famously referred to humans as *The Naked Ape*. Not only are we a 'naked' ape but we're also an aggressive one. How is this relevant in poker? Well, in many ways it is fundamental to your chances of playing well enough to win. That's because the battle that is a game of poker has traumatic effects on body language.

Simon Freedman is explicit about the role of aggression in his games of poker with friends: *'What it comes down to is enjoying the aggressive experience. In many ways it's like joking around with aggression. When you're with a group of friends you don't thump them or kick them but there's an underlying aggression there. Poker is a way of doing it in a controlled way. It's like teenagers play-fighting or stags interlocking horns.'*

YOUR THREE VOICES

Throughout most of your life you've been listening to three internal voices:

- *The instinctive voice*: This is the voice of survival and 'fight or flight'.
- *The social voice*: This is the voice of empathy and nurture.
- *The logical voice*: This is the voice of reason and rationality.

Babies and small children only hear the first one, making them egocentric, that is concerned with their own needs and wants. The other two are 'learned behaviours'. In this chapter we're looking at the way that first voice can still dominate and why.

What Simon Freedman refers to as aggression is *controlled* during play. So the last, logical voice must take careful charge of the first, instinctive one during a game of poker. As Simon adds: *'People that lose poker are people who lose their temper. You get into arguments about the pizza or whatever and these arguments turn into a big thing.'*

WINNING THE BATTLE

The words 'win' and 'lose' provide the clue to poker-play psychology. If you win or lose then you must have first been in a conflict. Your desire to win and what fuels it will affect every part of your play, sometimes positively but often negatively. By playing poker you're feeding a very basic desire to fight other animals.

Like all forms of warfare, from hand-to-hand fighting to military strategy, the victors are the ones who keep a cool head. They'll take a very primal, instinctive need and turn it into logic and created calm. Hotheads have their moment in the sun but hothead behaviour is only effective in surprise attacks. That surge of angry energy only gets one go at defeating an opponent. After that it's downhill all the way.

So why fight?

Animals fight over two key things: status and territory. Humans, too, are strongly hierarchical and territorial. We fight over both on a regular basis. By understanding your own aggressive and competitive motivators you will be able to suppress them more easily. If you ignore these very strong impulses you'll either be baffled by your own playing decisions that are prompted by them or you'll attempt to rationalise them, telling yourself that they're useful.

AGGRESSIVE AROUSAL

When you sit down to play poker you're in many ways like any other ape gearing up to fight. When you become aggressively aroused, the automatic nervous system kicks in. However, as we'll see in Chapter 6, which is all about stress, that system is kept in check by a balance between sympathetic and parasympathetic sub-systems. One eggs you on and the other urges you to calm down and reserve your strength.

When you fight, your body stops listening to the calming

parasympathetic system and lets the sympathetic take over. You gear up for action with any of the following:

- A burst of adrenaline.
- Changes in breathing patterns.
- Disruption to your digestion.
- Alterations to your style of movement.
- Your hair standing on end.

One added factor of this process that is hugely seductive for the average poker player is that when the sympathetic nervous system is in control you feel wide awake and full of energy. So far so good. But in any battle an opponent can also produce a response of fear. They might beat us. We immediately fall into a contradictory state with aggression driving us to fight and fear holding us back.

What this leads most animals to do is to start by *threatening* to attack. If an animal looks strong enough and formidable enough the opponent might back down. This is called 'ritualised combat'. In many ways, poker is an example of ritualised combat. A key skill of poker is bluffing, that is looking so confident or intimidating that your opponent backs down before blood is spilled (figuratively speaking, of course).

Watch other players as they arrive for a game and see the obvious displays of testosterone as they chat over drinks: legs are splayed wide, hand movements are exaggerated, there are subtle hand-to-chest gestures, and the laughter is louder and more raucous than usual. When male poker players meet there are often exaggerated rituals of patting that border on punching and much of the social discussion sounds like boasting.

Where do women fit into this framework? Not via the old laddish thumping rituals and that's a fact. Women employ their own combat techniques via flirting and financial or style put-downs. Or there can be those old, well-honed gestures of exasperation, like eye-rolling, tutting or mouth-pursing.

But the process of 'ritualised combat' is a complex one and as the game gets under way the stakes start to rise. As a player, you'll be experiencing all the symptoms prompted by the sympathetic nervous system. Then, once the 'battle' is over, your parasympathetic nervous system kicks in, calming you down and restoring balance.

When the sympathetic system is suppressed, though, there is often a swing between both systems. This means you can be flushed one minute and white-faced the next, breathing rhythms get interrupted, prompting us to puff and sigh, and the bladder that was closed for the fight suddenly wants to empty on a very urgent basis. Poker players have to cope with, suppress, or mask a whole range of conflicting symptoms as the game goes on, particularly if they are winning well or losing badly. This 'intrapersonal' struggle is fascinating to watch but uncomfortable and challenging to deal with – more challenging than most players realise, even experienced ones.

FIGHT OR FLIGHT BODY LANGUAGE

Of course, this swing between sympathetic and parasympathetic systems also has a dramatic effect on your body language. In animal terms, the effect of the two produces all the signals of ritualised combat that we can see on nature programmes – and on most high streets on a Saturday night once the pubs are shut. They consist of mock attacks and what look like dance rituals. Opponents strut their stuff to intimidate and so avoid physical conflict, then walk away as the parasympathetic system takes over.

ONLINE CONFLICT

You will also see and suffer these ritualised combat rituals when you sit at a poker table or even play online. Watch the body language power-posturing that takes place. But remember to monitor your own body language for signs of fight ritual.

When you play online it's very tempting to power-posture via the chat box, belittling or joking about your opponents. Even if you believe you only do this as a joke, remember, it's also a form of psychological sparring.

DISPLACEMENT ACTIVITIES

Another set of signals that can be confusing until you learn to understand what's occurring are what are called 'displacement activities'. These are unconscious gestures we use to displace the nervous energy caused by being unable to reveal how we really feel. Usually they are performed at moments of inner conflict or frustration. The suppression of genuine fight will lead animals and humans to perform what are often strange and irrelevant-looking body language rituals.

Apes often break off from aggressive power-posturing to eat, scratch or groom. Displacement gestures may even resemble sleep behaviour. The ape may yawn or close its eyes or mime nest-building, stacking twigs or throwing things into piles.

Humans have their own displacement activities, which vary from person to person. In many ways they are pointless apart from being a way to displace energy. Ties and hair that are already straight or tidy get re-straightened and re-tidied. Makeup gets checked and retouched. Nails are bitten, hair is twiddled and cuffs are fiddled with.

Prince Charles's side-pocket-patting, cuff-straightening and chest-pocket-checking rituals are nothing to do with searching for his keys or wallet, or adjusting clothing. He has a driver, he doesn't carry a wallet and his cuffs are immaculate, so the gestures are prompted by emotion, not need. Common displacement gestures include scratching, rubbing, nose-touching, throat-clearing, groaning and gurgling.

These rituals are familiar to poker players. Unless you identify that your opponents are employing displacement gestures, you could easily imagine they are bored because their hand is weak or bluffing bored to pretend their hand is weaker than it is. And when you yawn or scratch as you wait to play you could be giving away more clues about your hand and your emotional state than you realise.

Like any form of body language, gesture displacement activity has to be seen in context to uncover the likely meaning. If you think chip-stacking, yawning or nibbling food equals bored or uninterested you could make an expensive mistake.

It could be a bluff but it could also be displacement activity. The first will probably be part of a longer routine. The second, being the visible sign of the struggle between sympathetic and parasympathetic systems, will probably be erratic and sandwiched between more aggressive signals such as staring or sitting upright. But we'll examine this in more detail in Part Two when we study your opponents' play.

PSEUDO-FIGHT GESTURES

We humans have our own set of pseudo-fight gestures that we use when we're feeling aggressive and the sympathetic/para-sympathetic reactions kick in. Often we have no idea that we're using them, which is why they can be potentially revealing in poker. They include:

Fists

When we're suppressing aggression our hands start to curl into fists. In more open fights we use this as a power-posture, even shaking fists at our enemies.

Hand on the hip/elbow out

This is a relative of the body-puffing, chest-banging, hair-standing-on-end responses that apes use to look bigger. In humans it could emerge as placing hands behind head with elbows stuck out or even stretching to temporarily increase body size.

Loser behaviour

When an ape loses a fight it will usually signal total submission to avoid getting pulped and then run away. But sometimes it is unable to escape. So it needs to signal submission in a way that doesn't involve doing the obvious. When you sit around a poker table you are like a trapped ape. When your hand is weak your natural instinct is to slink off quietly with your tail between your legs. But poker rituals mean you have to stay in your seat. Often you have to stay there and pretend you're not a loser.

Keep an eye out for your own and others' appeasement gestures. Many of these will be as misleading or suppressed as the signals of aggression. But if you spot them by seeing them in the context of other body language clues you could have a strong insight into your opponents' psyche.

A losing ape will often hold out its hand to the winner. Because this risks getting it bitten, it signals an end to the conflict. In human terms this has become the ritual known as the loser's handshake, defeated players making themselves symbolically 'vulnerable' to the victor in a bid to end the fight.

You only get this signal – if at all – at the end of a tournament. There is then a lightening of tension because everyone knows the fight is ended. However, you might spot unconscious versions of the 'loser's handshake' during play. A 'loser' – that is someone who knows he has a weak hand – can often be spotted by a small palm-up begging gesture, especially if the hand moves towards the 'winner'. Be aware of your own hands too. Any palms-turned-upwards gestures might be leaking subconscious submission signals to your opponents.

Flirting

In animal behaviour, flirting is not just about sex. Flirting is also used as a 'de-motivation gesture' or 'appeasement signal', to defuse a potential threat from a dominant animal. When we flirt at work we're not necessarily vying for a date. More often we're just trying to boost the status of our bosses and so avoid being bullied.

Now an ape might do this by bending over and showing its bottom. You're unlikely to employ behaviour like this at the poker table. But other forms of mild flirting are common during a game and can signal play submission, especially if performed at a crucial moment in the game.

Baby-face

Another animal appeasement sign, juvenile behaviour aims to make the animal under attack appear helpless and non-aggressive.

Humans employ baby voices and 'cute' gestures and facial expressions in a bid to defuse a threat. I've seen business professionals use childlike signals when under pressure from a potentially hostile audience. When you see these at the poker table you can assume the player using them feels under threat. These signals can include any of the following:

- Shy smiles.
- Toes pointed together.
- Twisting hands together.
- Giggling.
- Dropping the chin.
- Legs crossed when standing.
- Flapping hands.
- Eye-rolling.
- Covering face with hands.
- Hands clasped behind back.
- Small bow or curtsey.
- Baby voices.

POKER FACE AND AGGRESSION

When we see a player employing stillness and quiet during a game it's easy to assume they're performing their poker face, refraining from using expressions, movement or chat so as to give nothing away to their opponents.

But apes also use stillness as an act of appeasement. When they feel under threat they may switch off any signals that might have been triggering aggression in another ape and also signal nonaggression on their own part. They may lower their body in order to look smaller and more submissive, or may even turn their face away. So if a player becomes subdued and visually 'quiet' it need not be a poker face. Keep in mind that they might genuinely be losing and under attack from a stronger player.

An ape might also use a reverse form of 'mirroring'. If the challenging ape looks down, the appeasing ape can raise its head upwards. If the angry ape has sticking-up hair the appeasing ape may flatten its own to signal submission. You could look for any of these appeasement rituals, however subtle, around your poker table. If you do, assume the one doing the appeasing is probably holding a weak hand, no matter how hard they might be trying to bluff with the rest of their body language.

So when you're playing poker always be aware of your 'animal potential'. By using information from this chapter to understand your own subliminal impulses you'll find it easier to harness and control them. That way you'll be suppressing your 'instinctive voice' and allowing your 'logical voice' to take its place.

4

MAKING THE LIE

There's probably no such thing as an honest poker player. By taking part in the game you are tacitly admitting your intention to lie to the other players. This is known as the 'agreed lie'. You know you'll lie. They know you'll lie. This creates an almost unique 'lie' scenario. Your opponents are expecting you to bluff. What they don't know is *how* or *when* you're going to do it.

Are you a good liar or a bad liar? It sounds odd to boast about your ability to deceive and fool people but those are the skills we're trying to perfect in this part of the book. In many ways, what goes on around the poker table is a lot like what goes on in real life, especially in the workplace. I have sat at many a boardroom table watching business discussions and thinking we're only a pack of cards away from a poker game. The masks are the same and the bluffing is just as strong. The negotiation might be over a contract or budget but the game is played in much the same way, with many of the same rituals. So, even if you don't actually play poker you'll be able to use the advice in this book to enhance your workplace skills.

Ladbrokes Poker Million winner John Duthie made a conscious effort to hone his skills: *'I don't think I am a naturally deceptive person, but I do appear to have the ability to be so when required. I don't think I use it a lot at work, but I am acutely aware when I do not believe a performance that an actor delivers.'*

POKER LIES

The chances are that if you think you're a good liar or even boast about your talent then you're not. A really good liar will understand the complexity of the skills involved and the need to continue to hone and evolve them. We humans are much better at judging others' behaviour than we are at judging ourselves. This is because we're dependent on others and their co-operation for our own survival.

We stand a better chance of survival if we live and work in a social group or pack. Therefore we have to be good at detecting behaviour. Now, while it can be logical to tell lies (why stick to the truth when you know it can get you into trouble or create more effort?) it also creates an unbelievable amount of pressure.

Why is this? Well, when you perform a lie your body must go though a very complex series of thinking and behaviours, proving why it's not easy, even for a consummate actor. There are strong pressures that make honesty a preferred option. To lie knowingly and deliberately requires a colossal mental effort. When we do this there is a formidable response in the brain.

Research at Sheffield University shows that each time we lie we have to stifle our automatic, instinctive responses, suggesting that it's natural to tell the truth and that it takes much more effort to lie. In order to tell a simple lie your brain has to go through three key stages:

- *Step one*: First it has to come up with the correct, honest response.
- *Step two*: Then it has to suppress it.
- *Step three*: Then it has to come up with the lie response.

All this is not only hard to do but also hard to sustain. Now, imagine your lies are only small ones – a little tactful massaging of the truth. Your partner asks if he's going bald, or if she's getting fat. You know there is only one correct answer for both scenarios and that is 'No'. So you say 'No' even though he could make a billiard ball look hirsute or she could fit Dawn French into one leg of her jeans.

Now, the pressure as you perform these lies will be intense. You not only know you need to lie but you also know that if you look as though you're fibbing you'll suffer the wrath of the paranoid partner anyway. In your favour, though, are two key facts:

- You've probably had loads of practice for this one and,
- The person you're lying to wants to believe you're telling the truth.

Now look at the poker lie. For a start, everyone you're playing is trying to discover whether you're bluffing or not. Then there's the fact that if you're staring at either a very poor hand or a very strong one you'll be feeling either euphoria or depression that will be trying to defy your attempts to suppress it. And finally, your bluffing performance is harder because you'll be feigning a subtle response, that is mild uninterest, boredom or even excitement.

In real life, as opposed to a poker game, our lies are usually 'unagreed'. We use them to manipulate, con, avoid punishment or argument, flatter or be tactful. The main objective of the 'unagreed lie' is to avoid letting on that we're lying. But in poker everyone knows or suspects. So the skills tend to be different. When you sit at a poker table the air is thick with non-verbal communication. Players are either trying to mask their emotions to conceal their hand or they're performing a bluff. But while you're masking you're also busy reading, trying to glean information from those other players that might give clues to their chances of beating you.

If you're not masking you could be performing, trying to misdirect by displaying signals that are opposite to your true feelings. Or you could even be performing the double-bluff, displaying accurate signals in the hope everyone will think you're bluffing. Of course you could play poker straight. No bluffs, no body language, just luck and logic. Poker without the bluffing and deceit is like sex with a condom: safer and less messy but not the same as the real thing.

WHY BLUFF?

Bluffing can win a game of poker. And I'm not just talking about the Oscar-winning performance bluffs, either. When opponents are making a poker decision they can be easily swayed. Even expert players have a certain degree of randomness in their calls. Unless the hand they're holding is very bad or very good their brain will be making decisions based on logic, statistics and something called the 'AF-factor'.

The AF-factor
This is where the randomness really kicks in. The AF-factor is 'affected behaviour'. In other words, a betting or playing decision

can be influenced by many things, including – or especially – you. It would be good to think that our poker decisions are purely objective. But even in this age of computer-logic that's extremely unlikely. Poker is an emotional game. What we bring to the table is a whole lot more than just some chips (or matchsticks if you're not playing for money) and a bowl of Pringles.

When your opponents are making a betting decision they can be swayed or affected in that decision by your behaviour. A frown, sigh, yawn or laugh will all penetrate their conscious or subconscious, adding to the rich and heady brew that is already bubbling away there. Keep this in mind when you're playing poker. If you take control of your own body language signals at the poker table you increase your power over the game. Much of that power comes from the AF-factor, your ability to sway your opponents' playing decisions.

The lie process

Lying is a two-way process. To be a great liar the people you are talking to must *want* to believe you. The lie then grows on a bed of collusion. When your audience wants to believe you they will look for positive signals and try to disregard the negatives.

If your partner has an affair you will want to believe the lie that nothing at all happened and you are the only love of their life. A mistress will want to believe that her married lover doesn't really care for his wife. When you hire a builder you want to believe that he is honest and trustworthy. Psychologists call this the 'truth bias'.

Truth bias

In modern life we're so busy and so overflowing with stimulus from work and recreation that we have little time to spend on spotting liars. So we tend to accept everything at face value until proven otherwise. When a salesperson tells you their product will achieve miracles you want to believe the patter. When an overweight person reads a book that offers an effortless weight-loss plan they want to believe what logic says must be illusion.

There are even times in our lives when we create a lie on behalf of someone else. This is called 'crooked listening', bypassing your natural ability to 'read' the signs in order to allow yourself to be fooled. A doctor may be breaking bad news to you but you're only listening for a positive prognosis and your mind converts the actual message into an 'ideal' one. Your partner is trying to dump you but you misinterpret their signals as undying devotion, as this is the 'truth' you prefer. Your boss gives you a bad appraisal but you take away the message that he or she is only jealous or feels threatened by your ability.

In poker, though, there is no place for 'crooked listening'. Your ability to lie and to read the lies of others is condensed into its purest form for the most basic of reasons: survival. Whether you're competing with money or not, forget the idea that you're playing for fun. You're taking part in a battle for power and superiority. By introducing money and bets you only intensify the gladiatorial element.

So what makes it so hard to deceive other people? When we fight for survival we become instinctively good at picking out liars. But the survival instinct doesn't help us to perform better lies. In fact, the survival instinct makes us very bad liars. The more the lie matters the less well we act. The very pressure of the moment makes the kind of body language nonchalance that would occur when we tell the truth a virtual impossibility.

HOW TO BE GOOD

To be an excellent body language liar you would have to either:

- Not care.
- Lie on a regular basis.
- Have been told when your lies have failed to work.

I put that last point in because it needs to be said that men and women tend to have different hit rates for their lying. The man might have the ability to excel at point one. Men still dominate in industry and politics and both cultures rate the ability to lie well as not just a necessity but as a quality for success. In politics especially, the need to lie can seem endemic and the term 'spinocchio' has been coined to mean a combination of political 'spin' and 'lie-telling'.

This linking of lying with success will often take away much of the associated guilt. If lying is linked to dominance and Alpha male/female superiority it means you care less about the moral implications. We know people in the legal profession have to become adept liars, as do shop workers and beauty workers. Selling, marketing and negotiating all require the ability to lie. When women talk to other women they tend to tell 'kind lies' to flatter them and avoid hurting their feelings. When they talk to men they tend to use more selfish lies – and so do men.

There are many professions that involve lying on a regular basis. But not all lies are prompted by self-gain. Nurses and carers are often called upon to make tactful lies. As are other workers who deal regularly with the public.

Regular bouts of lying like this will hone our skills and make the act of lying more and more comfortable for us. The 'caring' or 'tactful' liar who works in the medical or customer-facing professions will struggle more with the self-gain lie as the guilt is more likely to trip in than it would with someone who has squared up to self-gain lies professionally and absolved themselves of most or any associated guilt.

Criminals should make the best liars but this isn't always the case. I recently worked on a TV programme that used hidden cameras to catch out crooked tradesmen. Many of them were very bad liars and could only depend on the collusion of their customers to get away with it. One crook used body language techniques that he must have preserved from the nursery, widening his eyes to the size of saucers and raising his eyebrows to claim he hadn't just stolen cash that we'd seen him take from a jar less than a minute before.

One 'tradesman' had obviously spotted his own lie deficiencies and had attempted to cover all his body language signals, refusing to use eye contact and keeping his head down and his hands stuffed into his pockets rather than give himself away.

Researchers at The University of Massachusetts discovered people made three lies for every 10 minutes of conversation. So the point is you probably do lie on a very regular basis anyway. It's just that you don't always know it. There are lies and lies. Big whoppers and small moments of tact. Sometimes we lie to get attention or to turn dreams into reality. Often we lie just for the hell of it.

When we lie throughout our lives our techniques usually get some sort of feedback or reward. In many ways our ability to lie or cheat well can rest on three factors:

- Upbringing.
- Peer pressure and the perceived need to please your peers.
- Immaturity.

By immaturity I'm referring to that state of egocentricity that children often exist in. It means attention-seeking and a lack of empathy for others. It means you believe you are the most important person in the universe and the only one who matters. This will in turn make you much more reckless and less likely to suffer feelings of guilt. Being self-centred will help to make you a more accomplished cheat or liar.

IT'S YOUR MOTHER'S FAULT

Small children lie a lot, usually from about the age of three or four. This is because of something psychologists call the 'magnified reward' – maximum reward for minimum effort. It's why small children love balloons so much, one tiny shove and something very big moves a very great distance. So children often find lying the easier option. If a child misbehaves the parent might not know. If the parent asks the child if they've done something wrong the child can be honest, in which case he or she is told off. So the next time they decide to lie and do not get told off. Sometimes the lie gets found out and they're told off anyway. So which to choose? The fact is that the likelihood of being told off is greater if the child tells the truth than if they lie. So the lie option is chosen through pure logic.

Lying can often seem a logical option in adulthood, too. Why bother studying for exams when a simple lie on your CV will have the same effect? Why buy a Mercedes to impress the girls when a simple lie that it's in the garage will impress for less? We could spend our lives taking what seems like the easy option. Yet many adults outgrow the 'magnified reward' effect during puberty, opting instead for the more satisfying hit that comes from delayed gratification, knowing you worked hard to achieve a goal.

Whether people continue to lie often depends on the effort involved in lying versus the reward it earns. Good liars were often confident children. For a confident child, lacking in anxiety or social diffidence, those early lies will have been easy to tell. Children start to mask their facial expressions and perform a more appropriate one from a very young age. Our parents will usually egg us on in this lie. We're told:

- 'Don't sit there with that long face.'
- 'Look grateful when your nan gives you a present.'
- 'Look as if you're pleased with that pullover.'
- 'Stop looking sulky.'
- 'Stop looking bored.'

Women can often tell when a partner lies but pretend to believe it. This makes men think they are good liars when they're not and to repeat what they believe are 'successful' techniques that are easy to see through. There are obvious advantages to this. If the man believes his lie has been swallowed he will never learn to hone or adapt his lie techniques.

PANIC

The stress of the lie performance can bring on bouts of panic, especially if you are an honest person by nature and feel that lying is wrong, even to be tactful. Panic is like an emotion over-ride. It cancels out all other feelings and behaviours, driving your pre-planned responses into melt-down. Panic blocks the fight–flight response. You want to opt for 'flight' but instead end up freezing like a rabbit caught in headlights.

To avoid this you need to learn how to avoid what psychologists call 'detection apprehension' – fear of being caught out in your lie or bluff. So the lesson to take with you to the poker table is this: lying might seem easy but it isn't. Underestimate the effort involved at your peril! Work on your bluffing techniques if you want to be convincing.

Social poker player Devlin Tagoe has seen what happens when the bluff is badly executed: *'I always try to read the other players but I have one friend who is obvious. He only ever plays aggressively when he's got a good hand. This is his style and he never changes it.'* Imagine the effect if Devlin's friend finally cottoned on to his over-regular behavioural give-away. One swift change on a key hand and he might walk away with the pot.

5

ARE YOU READY TO RUMBLE?

Body language is – by and large – the visible sign of your inner emotional state. Although it's possible to act out a lie or bluff, it's hard to sustain the performance for long periods. The longer you lie the more the truth tries to leak out. Better, then, to feed your body language with as many statements of fact as possible. You can do this by creating positive thoughts that make your poker performances less of a stretch.

EMOTIONAL BAGGAGE

When you take your seat at the poker table you bring some emotional baggage with you. With some players it's just hand luggage but others drag in whole suitcases. It is made up of your inner thoughts and feelings created by past experience and it will affect your poker performances unless you make yourself aware of it. Your emotional baggage can contain any or all of the following:

- Pride.
- Fear.
- Confidence – or lack of it.
- Being bullied at school.
- Wanting to be liked.
- Alpha male/female desire to assert natural colony authority.
- Being a bad loser.
- Being a bad winner.
- Social embarrassment.
- The belief that you are 'lucky' or 'unlucky'.
- The belief that you have a natural instinct for sniffing out a win.
- A feeling you might be psychic.
- A hatred of the rest of the world.
- Parents who always gave you what you wanted on demand.
- Parents who made you wait or earn gifts or favours.
- An older sibling.
- A younger sibling.
- No siblings.
- A desire to boast about the money you have.
- A good sex life.
- A lousy sex life.
- A short attention span.
- A craving for excitement.
- A love of risk-taking.
- A desire to avoid risks.

Get it? Almost anything from your past and present – and even anticipated future – can become a self-induced affected behaviour – the 'AF-factor'. So how does this awareness help you when you're playing?

John Duthie explains: *'There are times when I feel super-confident and times when I don't. I do believe that my state of mind is reflected in my body language and if you exhibit any form of weakness at the poker table then I am afraid it gets pounced upon and you may as well leave and play another day. All good players are very aware of your personal mental state and are constantly looking for ways to capitalise on it. If you suffer a bad beating then the players are aware of this and will try to destroy you and your confidence. I am afraid that I do the same myself because this is the arena I put myself in and some days I suffer and others I don't.'*

Your emotional baggage shapes your behaviour. It influences your choices and decisions. Every move you make in a game of poker will be influenced by your emotions in one way or another – and so it is important to be aware of this fact.

Your past history makes you the kind of player that you are today. What you have to decide is this: Do you also want it to make you the kind of player you are tomorrow?

MOTIVATIONAL FACTORS

You might think you understand your own motivational factors for winning at poker but it will still be useful to question or examine them before you get stuck into your techniques. Never assume the obvious. Knowing your true self is never 'a given'.

Knowing what really motivates you is essential for poker success. Why? Because, whether we like it or not, your behaviour is linked to your most basic motivational factors. Did you ever sit trying to study for an exam or finish a piece of important work but find that your mind refused to co-operate? Did you ever have an important job interview but discovered to your horror that you were going to be late? When our goals are out of kilter with our true motivational factors it's often the motivators that take charge of our behaviour.

I once co-wrote a book called *The Tall Poppy*. This is a syndrome that is well known in sporting circles and the celebrity world. It defines the way a player or celeb becomes successful and famous only to be knocked down by the public that had previously supported them. It's as though you are destroyed for over-stepping the mark.

This happens at school. Clever kids are popular up to the point where they become too smart. Then the other kids go off them. If these children are exceptionally good even the teachers may dislike them. I call this the 'Tall Poppy Syndrome', that is being cut down to size once you've grown taller than all the other flowers.

What I discovered during my research is that the 'Tall Poppy Syndrome' can be self-inflicted. Who would want to do that? you might well ask. How many footballers destroy what is an apparently 'ideal' career by boozing and partying? How many successful politicians have ruined a promising future by cheating on their wives or taking midnight strolls across a park?

Did you ever think that some of them were almost begging to be caught out? Perhaps that is the right conclusion. Maybe their behaviour is a sign that they've been reaching for the wrong goals. Perhaps they were led by a need to impress other people but not themselves. Success is difficult to achieve if it's not compatible with your own motivational factors. The same will be true of your attempts to achieve success at poker. How you play will be dominated by your inner psyche. Before you can play well you need to know not only that you want to win, but also *why*.

ARE YOU READY TO RUMBLE?

To be consistently good at poker you must ask yourself the following questions and be honest with the answers:

- Do I want to win?
- Do I *really* want to win?
- Do I want to win the biggest pot?
- Do I want to beat other people?
- Do I ever play hoping to lose?

That last question might sound bonkers. In fact several of these questions might sound potty – but dig deep. It's worth a few moments navel-gazing before you answer them. Nobody likes to lose. That sounds like a given. But there is losing and *losing*. Sometimes what feels like, looks like, smells like and tastes like a win can really be a lose if the 'win' worked in contradiction to your core motivational factors.

How so? Well winning, as we know, brings its own problems. Your subconscious might be aware of these problems and try to sabotage your 'win'. For instance, winning money or a competition can make you unpopular. Others might get jealous or bitter. Did you ever 'win' promotion at work? How many of your colleagues looked *really* pleased for you? By promoting the win you can become less popular and even alienated from the group. 'Tough!' you might cry. But never forget that one of the basic human instincts is to be liked and accepted. So now let's look at some of the key motivational factors.

Relationships

Perhaps your key motivational factor is relationships. You like company and you enjoy the social side of poker. In many ways you like to be liked. Fine. But this may mean you're better off playing fun poker with friends for a small pot or no money at all. When big sums change hands personal popularity flies out of the window. Big wins are all about respect, not love.

Attention-seeking

You might be motivated by the desire to seek attention. All that betting and winning will work for you because during moments of high tension, when you're in the game right to the end, all eyes are on you. Fine. But what about once you've won? Other players may feel embarrassed and pay less attention to you. Perhaps a loser gets all the attention and sympathy. If you got maximum attention as a child when you fell over and hurt yourself you might sabotage a potential poker win in order to gain sympathy attention.

The entertainer

Your key motivational factor might be fun. Perhaps you love to be the centre of attention as an entertainer. You like to crack jokes all the time and perform. You're never happier than when the spotlight's on you. Again, fine. But how would you handle a top tournament when a poker face is called for, rather than an acted bluff? How will you keep the jokes down when you need to play at being serious? Again, your motivational desires could mean you never achieve the poker wins that you thought you were aiming for.

Money

You might want to work towards the 'win' but why? Winning money might sound like an easy answer but money isn't a motivator. Money moves people and makes them do things such as a day's work but it doesn't motivate them to enjoy that work. If a job's miserable it's still miserable even if you're given more money to do it. The initial burst of pleasure at the pay rise won't make the job any nicer.

So you're more likely to be motivated by the feeling of power or status that accompanies the win and the money it rewards you with. By winning the pot you prove your tribal supremacy. The evidence for this lies in the body language signals that most non-professional players use when they've won the pot. Instead of sliding the chips across the table towards them there is often some form of chest-beating gesture that signals to all the other players around the table that there's a new Alpha male/female in the room.

CHANGE OF MOTIVATORS?

So now you know the bad news. If a poker win isn't compatible with your core motivational factors the chances are you'll self-combust and ruin any chances of winning. Maybe not in a big or dramatic way, but in a lesser 'sick note' fashion such as:

'I didn't feel lucky tonight.'
'I just couldn't keep my poker face up. I knew they'd sussed me.'
'I was hung over.'
'I got nervous.'
'I was too drunk.'
'My opponent was on a roll.'

You have some options here. You can stick with what you enjoy. You stay true to yourself and keep to your basic motivators. You enjoy the fun. You chat to your mates. You carry on gaining as much social reward from the loss as you do from the occasional win. You don't push yourself beyond that motivational reward system.

What price words like 'fun' and 'mates' then? Success comes with its own pressures and stress. Alternatively you embrace those pressures and allow your goals to exceed your motivators. You knowingly forgo the fun factor or the safety and comfort of losing to try your hand at some serious wins. If you've chosen the second option your next steps will be:

- Awareness of your problem and the size of it.
- Plan some re-motivating.

Imagine you won the lottery. How great would that be? Well, not very great in reality. You'd begin to doubt the motives of your friends and any new acquaintances. You'd have the stress of new purchases and investments. Your marriage could break down under the strain.

Now, by keeping yourself on track with your motivators you could avoid some of these problems. In poker it's even easier. What you must do is visualise what the win will look like and feel like in reality. You need to be aware of the negative results such as unpopularity or even the feeling of ruthlessness that could be alien to your nature. To progress beyond the fun games you may need to create a clear division to cope, if you're motivated by relationships or performance attention. Shore up these values in another way. Find another outlet for your friendships or performing.

Next you'll need to work on overcoming the symptoms and behaviours that an urge to win-scupper is producing. In Chapter 3 we looked at the triangular process of Think–Feel–Behave. Your core motivators will have a profound effect on your thinking and, in turn, affect the way you play poker. Nothing's more frustrating and annoying than the feeling that you're allowing yourself to play badly or lose games. Sometimes it is all down to luck. Often it can be the 'Tall Poppy Syndrome'.

To improve your game then and increase your chances of winning you need to take control of your thinking. 'Emotional baggage' creates negativity or emotionally instinctive play decisions. These are most dangerous when you're in denial and unaware they're occurring. By tagging your thoughts and telling yourself how you would like to be thinking – that is, clear, calm, logical, unemotional, positive – you can change the direction of your play to produce winning behaviours.

Think smart

To become a good body language performer you're going to have to start by taking control of your thinking. Imagine your brain is a busy road junction. Thoughts come and thoughts go. They need to be processed and redirected along with the external messages. If you allow your thoughts to descend into disorder and chaos the result will be disaster. Allowing your mind to think in an impulsive and reactive way when you're put under pressure to perform will be similarly disastrous, like setting all the traffic lights to green.

Once a thought has been allowed to pop up into your head it will be like a grenade with the pin out. That thought will start to have an effect on your feelings. Those newly created feelings will then set about influencing your behaviour. So if your first thought was negative your performance will be rubbish. However, if you 'edit' your thoughts your performance will improve and your body language signals will begin to help rather than hinder your cause.

In the theatre this is called method acting, taking on the thoughts of the character you're trying to portray and then translating those feelings and emotions into a physical performance. All you need to do is establish a few 'thinking' rules.

Tag your thoughts

Capture each thought as it enters your head and create a 'tag' for it to define its usefulness or not. 'Tagging' means creating a mental label for each idea so that it can be re-allocated or dumped. Some negative thoughts may recur. But just make sure you dump them as often as they pop up into your mind.

Challenge assumptions

If you keep telling yourself 'I'm a bad liar' or 'I'm always unlucky at cards' you're creating a self-fulfilling prophecy. When negative inner dialogues like this pop into your mind you must become your own traffic cop. Make them stop and then redirect them somewhere else. If you allow them access they'll erode your confidence in the skills you need to succeed. Anyone who thinks they're a bad liar will feel nervous or anxious about creating the lie and their body language performance will suffer.

ARE YOU READY TO RUMBLE?

Get rid of NID

NID stands for 'negative inner dialogues'. When you communicate with others there are two voices involved:

- *Interpersonal*: Communication with the other person, and
- *Intrapersonal*: Communication with yourself.

It's difficult to communicate well if your intrapersonal dialogues are sabotaging you. Or, to put it another way, don't allow your self-talk to talk yourself down.

When you play a game of poker, everyone around that table is pitted against you. They all want you to lose. (Unless you're playing your mum.) Now, assuming you have nothing but opponents sitting around you, how dumb would it be to add to their number with a negative voice in your own head? Surely you need someone on your side? When you play poker you need a coach, minder, best pal and personal psychiatrist all on tap. And unless you're as rich as Bill Gates I doubt you play with an entourage. Which means you'll have to supply all these services yourself.

Here are some examples of NID dialogues that you need to dump:

'I was never good at acting.'
'I barely understand the rules.'
'I'm not as ruthless as this lot.'
'I'm so nervous I can barely remember my own name, let alone work out what cards the other players have got.'
'I never win anything.'
'I can't afford to lose.'
'They all look more experienced.'
'I just know I'm going to lose tonight.'

'I have no idea how to play this hand.'
'I'm sure that guy opposite can see right through me.'
'I have noodles for brains.'

Give new ideas access

Now you need to supply alternatives. Write down some 'ideal' messages before you play. If you get stuck, imagine you're coaching a new player. They have the same amount of experience as you but they're de-motivated. In other words, you'll need to send some positive thoughts zipping along your new super-highway. For example, 'I am learning to become an accomplished performer' would be good, as would thoughts such as 'I enjoy the excitement of acting a role' or 'I am now more perceptive about other players' signals.'

You could also say things like:

'Focus on the win.'
'I know I can stay calm under pressure.'
'The others are good but I will be better.'
'I have a great memory.'
'Go for it!'
'Seize the day!'

Statements like these are called 'positive affirmations'. They self-motivate and help place you in the 'thinking' state you need to be in to be a winner. Remember, though, these thoughts don't replace talent, planning and practice. Positive thinking became popular in the 1980s but in the business world some wires got crossed and the messages became translated into 'You can achieve anything if you tell yourself you're good.' This is the mantra of the terminally lazy and the loser.

ARE YOU READY TO RUMBLE?

To work, positive affirmations must sit neatly on top of dedication, practice and hard work. They add that extra spurt by freeing your body or your talent from its shackles of modesty, negativity, doubt or low self-esteem. Combine positive affirmations with talent and hard work and the possibilities are endless.

POSITIVE VISUALISATIONS

Once you've revved yourself up with positive self-talk you can begin to rehearse your game by visual techniques. Visualisations aren't new but they are effective. Simply see yourself doing well in your own imagination. This creates a feeling of confidence and 'winner mentality' plus a physical identification with winning. Your imagination is incredibly powerful and harnessing it to play poker can only be for the good. First let me convince you of the power of your imagination.

Have you ever cried at a movie like *Bambi* or *Titanic*? While you were blubbing were you not aware on a conscious level that Bambi is a sketch on paper and that Kate Winslet and Leonardo DiCaprio are highly paid Hollywood stars, neither of whom drowned on board an ocean liner over 90 years ago? Of course you knew this in your conscious mind but your subconscious still responded to the image in front of it, taking it literally. In other words it was easily fooled.

When you create positive visualisations in your imagination you achieve the same trick of fooling your subconscious into producing an emotional response. In this case you're looking to create feelings of confidence and win potential.

It doesn't take long to learn to use visualisation. All you need is some quiet time alone with no distractions. Once you get the hang of visualising you'll find you can do it in the middle of a crowded room. Here's how you do it:

Close your eyes and blank out your mind. Do this by focusing on the sound of your own breathing and imagine you're sitting in a huge empty cinema, gazing at a blank screen. Stare at the darkness for a few moments and try to empty your mind. (Don't worry if thoughts keep intruding, just keep listening to your own breathing until you achieve a partial mental space.)

Start to build a mental image of yourself playing poker. This is going to be the 'ideal' self, playing confidently and assertively in the style you would like to use. The hands are going in your favour but not so much that you can afford to just sit back and win. To win you will have to bluff. You enjoy the performance and the other players are totally taken in by it.

Every time you bluff you win the pot. No one has even noticed you're bluffing, that's how good you are. You know you've cracked the technique and you know you can use it whenever and however you want. You have no self-doubt. As long as the cards are good, so is your game.

Really feel what this 'winning you' feels like and immerse yourself in the emotion while monitoring your own techniques. Feel the enjoyment and confidence. Watch your own body language as you bluff your way towards the win. Don't make it easy but make it possible.

BE MODEST

Modesty is an odd value, especially when applied to sport, performing or gambling. In everyday life it can make us seem appealing, but some psychologists therefore claim it is one of the most common forms of lying.

ARE YOU READY TO RUMBLE?

American psychologists Bryan Gibson and Daniel Sachau looked at the 'modesty' lie, claiming that self-deprecating behaviour is often a deliberate strategy to cleverly manipulate others. Modesty after a win shows a desire to be liked by avoiding looking better, more skilful or more clever than your opponents. 'Limping' is pretending to be much worse at something than you are in an attempt to get your opponents to underestimate your threat. 'Playing passive' is appearing helpless to get others to feel sorry for you. 'Self-scuppering' is creating an excuse for yourself in case you fail.

Talking yourself up is the new modesty. You hear people 'bigging themselves up' all the time in business. This technique caught on when it was described as 'creating future history' – that is, taking something that you want to be true and talking about it as though it is. This is a useful technique for quitting smoking. Saying 'I don't smoke' is a bold and affirming statement that might well fool the subconscious into agreeing. At any rate, the least it does is make you throw away your ciggies. I used the phrase 'I hate chocolate' and said it so often it helped cure a life-long addiction.

However, never replace diffidence with arrogance. By replacing ideas of doubt with over-egged thoughts of competence you'll find your performances will take a downturn as your ability is outstripped by over-confidence. Anyone who watches *The Apprentice* will know what I mean. Candidates make hugely exaggerated claims about their own talents, stating categorically that 'I am the best salesman'/'I am the top at business presentations'/'I always succeed in managing a team' and on and on, and then we watch as their words are proved to be nothing more than empty boasts.

Sports people talk themselves up. Muhammad Ali told everyone that he was 'the greatest' but he was a superb boxer who had trained and developed his techniques at the same time. When the football manager Jose Mourinho describes himself as 'The Chosen One' his confidence sits on top of truth and experience.

If a loser talks like a winner it's more likely that he or she won't bother to study their craft or hone their skills at the same time. If you build dialogues telling yourself that you're an ace at poker before you've got the skills you'll come a cropper. If you tell yourself to banish negative thoughts but replace them with realistic encouragement you'll not only feel better about your skills but you'll begin to look better too.

BECOME A LIE ENTHUSIAST

It's really no good pussyfooting around. If you're going to be a good poker performer then you're going to have to learn to love the lie. Natural distaste and guilt has to be offloaded because those are thoughts you don't need on your new super-highway. If you're going to lack the stomach for the job then you might as well take any idea of winning and throw it down the drain.

If you want to play poker for fun alone then that's great but remember how much more fun it is if you're winning. And always remember the fun you can have misleading others and reading others. Lightweights don't win poker games.

Prepare your lying well in advance

Bad liars get caught on the hop. An audience to a lie will tend to expect it to be knee-jerk or a response to being cornered or caught out. These defensive lies are usually transparent.

ARE YOU READY TO RUMBLE?

Historically our TV screens have been littered with episodes of this type of lying or question-deflecting. Former US President Bill Clinton sat square to camera telling the world that he had not had sex with Monica Lewinsky (a young intern with whom he was alleged to have had a relationship) but a viewer may think that his facial expressions and body language told another story.

Even emotional 'liars' discover problems when they get caught on the hop. When Labour leader Tony Blair addressed the Women's Institute, after he became Prime Minister, he got unexpectedly booed and heckled. His 'performed' response was to smile and look nonplussed but the way he reached for a glass of water and the change in his expression as he did so appeared to tell a very different story as his face dropped and his teeth clenched.

Politicians who try to stand up to tough interrogation from the likes of TV interviewer Jeremy Paxman also send out clear signals of panic and indecision before they attempt to 'pretend' all is well. When former Home Secretary Michael Howard famously received a Paxman grilling his calm verbal responses were given away by his eyes, which appeared to send out the message that he was under pressure.

US President George Bush has similar eye 'give-aways' when he's trying to go for the last-minute bluff. When a journalist quizzed him on the names of world leaders his performed gestures were intended to simulate humour and easy-going indifference to being caught out but his eyes darted and then froze at one vital moment, seemingly displaying inner turmoil and potential panic. When we attempt a last-minute lie the chances are we'll be fooling nobody.

Never lie to yourself

Be honest with yourself about what you don't know and what you can't do or work out. Bluffing yourself is not an option. Boasting to yourself is stupid. Signal-reading is all about risk-assessment.

Never 'just be yourself'

This is plain lazy. Work and hone your body language skills.

Optimist or pessimist?

Optimistic people tend to be more successful than pessimists. Why? Well they start with the expectation of success and so are far more likely to get stuck in and have a go. It also means they're less likely to quit at the first hurdle. Pessimists will often not try at all, or if they do it is just to prove it won't work. They expect a bad outcome so they have the wrong attitude and put in little effort.

So, optimism is key. But you need to keep in mind that there are two types of optimist:

- *The active optimist*: They'll want to win, maybe think a win is possible or even likely, but they'll work hard to earn their 'luck'. Whatever it takes.
- *The passive optimist*: These are the ones that pitch up on programmes like *The X Factor* and, devoid of all talent, claim with their last breath that they *will* be a star. They think fame is their God-given right and that they should do nothing at all to earn it, just show up and get indignant when they're turned down at the audition. Being a passive optimist will make you a very high-risk poker player indeed. You'll think the game

looks easy and you may even have some beginner's luck. But then you'll lose your house, your car, the clothes you stand up in and next thing you'll be in the queue for *The X Factor*, claiming you can sing like Madonna. Hey ho!

PHYSICAL PREPARATION

Actors prepare for a performance and you can prepare too. So what if your personal performance is all taking place around a poker table rather than a stage? Many great films have been written about the drama of the game and to be a truly great player you'll need to use physical skills that might test a Royal Shakespeare Company actor.

A poker player's 'warm-ups' are all about preparing body and mind. Earlier on I looked at revving up the brain to get focus and emotional direction. Now all you've got to do is work on that temple of thespian creativity, your body. Remember that the act of lying or bluffing affects the breathing, muscles and digestive system as you move into 'fight or flight' mode and the adrenaline buzz kicks in. The aim of the 'warm-up' is to suppress or minimise these responses so that you look and sound as normal as possible. Playing yourself might sound easy but to consciously replicate normal subconscious behaviours when things are not 'normal' can be difficult.

WARM-UPS

If you're anxious or excited at any time during the game it can be signalled by your breathing. As tension in the body rises the breathing becomes shallower and less frequent. Breathing warm-up exercises will help relax your body, voice and mind before the game. Breathing check-ups during the game will maintain this feeling of relaxation and help control any give-aways or leakage in your performance.

Breathing warm-ups

- *The cooling breath*: This is an instant calmer that is easy to do – provided you can roll your tongue. Poke your tongue out of your mouth and curl it into a roll so that the sides of the tongue are nearly touching. Use your tongue as a straw to breathe air in and out. This cools the body down and calms the breathing and the mind. If you're unable to roll your tongue, purse your lips instead, as though you're about to whistle.

- *The self-comforting breath*: Place one hand in front of your mouth at a distance of 10–12 cm (4–5 in) and blow gently on your fingertips. Breathe in through your nose and out through your mouth. This is a soothing exercise that also regulates your breath.

Humming

Humming has two key benefits: it raises the spirits and it warms up the voice. Start with a low, deep hum and bring it up higher and higher, feeling it work all the way up through your vocal cords and body.

Muscle flexers

Starting with your toes, tense and flex each muscle in your body slowly and carefully. You don't need to do this visibly, it's a technique you can use any time you're standing still or sitting down. By mentally visiting each part of your body in turn it also helps focus the mind.

ARE YOU READY TO RUMBLE?

Get into the zone

Leading athletes do this in the last few minutes before an event. It involves emptying the mind, rather than over-filling it with last-minute commands and information. Sit quietly, ideally after your muscle flexers, and close your eyes. See the darkness and immerse yourself in it. Blank out every thought (this is harder than you may think but do your best). Creating a mental gap like this helps re-boot the brain, sluicing out all the unnecessary thoughts and replacing them with positive energy and focus.

Facial massage

When you ask your face to create a 'mask' for your bluff it's easy to suffer from what I call the Botox Effect. This is a temporary freezing of the facial muscles that makes you talk as though sprayed with glue. This might sound like a winning 'poker face' but it's more surreal than realistic and reveals your anxiety. Actors suffer the same thing and you'll often see inexperienced presenters talking through a mouth that is as rigid as the hole in a pillar box. Even blinking looks painfully difficult.

Avoid this face-freeze by doing warm-ups just before you go into the room to play. A facial massage will get the ball rolling and also provide a feeling of absolute calm and relaxation. Use the pads of your fingers – the 'fingerprint' part, not the points. Spread your fingers and place them along the sides of your face, from ear to jaw, with the thumbs just under the chin. Massage gently, using small circular movements. Don't press hard, the effect is enhanced if you keep the pressure light. Next work your fingers along your hair line and then – if your hairstyle can stand it – work them gently into the scalp.

Now, using the thumb and index finger, gently 'pinch' the top of your nose between the eyes and massage carefully. Work upwards towards the 'frown' area above the eyebrows. Using the same gesture with both hands, 'pinch' your eyebrows gently and carefully massage them from one end to the other and then back again, several times. This will relax the muscles around your eyes. Using the fingertips again – with the very lightest of touches – gently massage beneath the eye, along the cheekbone from one end to the other. Close your eyes then go on to the next stage, which is . . .

Mouth workouts

Close your mouth and squeeze the lips into a pout. Hold for a few seconds then stretch the corners of the mouth out as wide as possible so that you appear to be wearing a very fixed-looking smile. Hold for the same amount of time, then go back to the pout. Repeat several times to relax the muscles around the mouth.

Letting your lower jaw drop gently, press the tip of your tongue into the roof of your mouth. Hold, relax, repeat. This gets rid of tension in your jaw. Imagine your jaw is like a ventriloquist's dummy. Sticking your lower teeth out slightly, raise and lower the jaw, making an 'Aw-Aw-Aw' sound as you do so. This also relaxes jaw tension.

Sitting upright, say every letter in the alphabet, exaggerating each mouth movement required as you do so. Repeat each letter six times, enunciating as clearly as possible: 'Ay-Ay-Ay-Ay-Ay-Ay-Bee-Bee-Bee-Bee-Bee-Bee-Cee-Cee-Cee-Cee-Cee-Cee' and so on.

Try all these warm-up techniques before you decide which ones you will use before your games. Forget embarrassment. Yes, I know they all sound very precious and may well make you laugh when you first do them but get over it! Do you want to play well or not? The only way you'll really look an idiot is if your voice starts quivering and your hands begin to shake when you get dealt that strong hand at the table and you lose out on the big pot because your leakage is so transparent.

MANAGING POKER STRESS

You can't predict the level or tension of play until you're well into the game, so it's easy for stress to catch you on the hop. Some stress is good. It's what gives you the adrenaline rush you need when you play. But you have to keep it under control. Otherwise stress can stop you thinking clearly and can also influence your body language, making it easy for your opponents to read your mental turmoil. Managing poker stress involves two stages:

- *Preparation*: To ensure you are in as calm a state as possible before the game, and
- *Maintenance*: To stay calm as the pressure mounts.

The advice in this chapter can prevent sudden bouts of stress response sabotaging your game.

POKER STRESS

Poker stress is relative. Some people thrive under huge amounts of pressure that would crush the rest of us while others go to pieces at the slightest setback. Before you launch yourself into 'serious' poker playing, I would strongly advise you to take the following course in stress management. Why? Well, several reasons:

- *Stress can catch you on the hop*: You might have been enjoying a few regular games, then suddenly your confidence ebbs and the pressure starts getting to you.
- *Stress can be self-inflicted*: Even if your opponents are laid-back about your playing you could turn into your own worst taskmaster and start beating yourself up for losing.
- *Stress affects your ability to bluff*: It changes your breathing patterns, blink rate, muscle tension and voice pitch – and that's just for starters.
- *Stress affects your intellectual abilities*: It can make you dumb, dumb, dumb. You need a cool head to remember what cards have already been dealt. But once you are stressed that cool head will desert you and you'll be bumping along the bottom playing on a mix of adrenaline and desperation.
- *Stress inhibits your ability to read your opponents*: Your anatomical thinking skills will 'lift up their skirts and take a hike out the door'.

WHAT IS STRESS?

Stress is a survival response and without it we'd be extinct. It kicks in when there is a threat of danger, making you momentarily more quick-witted, stronger and faster. Which all sounds fab if you're being chased by a lion. Most of this is caused by the sudden surge of adrenaline. This triggers a strong physical response:

- Shorter, shallower breathing to energise the body.
- Increased pulse rate to increase your reaction times.
- Excessive sweating to cool the body.
- Muscle tension to make you stronger.
- Digestive system shutdown to prioritise energy to the muscles.
- Bowel and bladder emptying to lighten your weight.

It's impossible to be stress-free, and because fear can focus the mind you may even find your play improves when you have a buzz of fear, anxiety or excitement pulsing through your system. In terms of clear-headed thinking it can't be beaten. Adrenaline creates a good sense of awareness. However, just as one cup of coffee can stimulate your mind, more than one can make you jittery and unable to think straight. Stress is the same. A little nerves might sharpen your game but too much will dull it.

When we're thinking clearly our conscious brain is able to access all the stored knowledge that we've packed away in the subconscious. Think of the subconscious as some kind of vast warehouse and you'd be along the right lines. A little anxiety can speed up the access. But too much can lead to stress causing those warehouse doors to close. Even simple actions become difficult. I once messed up my PIN number in a supermarket queue, purely because I *tried* to remember it rather than letting my fingers tap it out using 'muscle memory'. The card was refused and my brain went into meltdown. I allowed the pressure of the moment to create stress.

By the time I got home I was even questioning the code for my alarm system. I think I ended up trying to turn off my alarm using my PIN number. I was in a hurry and I self-pressured. What I should have done was to take a moment, think of nothing and allow my brain to cool down. When we self-pressure it's like flooding the engine when the car won't start. The best thing to do is switch off, wait a bit and try again.

How does this all affect your poker game? Well, to play winning poker your brain needs tuning up but not turning off. Excitement will tune it so that you're peaking happily, fully awake and aware and able to remember and keep track of other cards. It will also enable you to make good betting decisions that are based on patterns and pre-planning, not loads of emotional baggage. Logic and calm are good. Paranoia, power-posturing and taking silly risks are not.

Stress goggles

Things look different when you're stressed. What would normally be a very bad idea can appear sound when you're wearing stress goggles. Big risks seem tiny. It can look as though real life takes a breather and all bets are off, except for the ones you're making at that table. Wiping that smug smile off the other guy's face can appear much more important than having enough money to pay for your daughter's wedding or the dog's hip replacement. Okay, maybe I'm over-dramatising but I'm sure you get my drift.

BODY CONTROL

It is absolutely vital that you keep in mind the physical reactions to stress. We've already established that winning at poker can depend on good body control. Stress is the number one enemy of body control. Stress is a survival response. Body control is just something you try to adopt to win a game of cards. Manage stress before you get to the table, don't start wrestling with it while you're there.

We all have our own unique stress triggers and 'ideal' levels of pressure. Stress is also extremely whimsical. What you could take in your stride one day can trip you up the next. Top sports people know this and do everything they can to prevent it happening. Once their confidence goes their nerve goes too and it is one hell of a job to rebuild. If you're banking on being a top poker player you'll need a special kind of psyche that can gamble and lie without suffering from stress.

Sports people know all about harnessing the positive effects of anxiety. A swimming coach once described it to me as taking those butterflies in the stomach and making them 'fly in formation'. That's what you must do with your poker stress – make it fly instead of allowing it to go into freefall in what's termed a 'stress spiral'.

Another key word in stress management is 'perception' – perceiving something non-life-threatening as physically dangerous. This will happen to your game if you allow yourself to believe your opponents are special or scary. Which is why some of the top players dress to produce just that response. Eye shades, tinted glasses, cowboy gear, gangster clothes . . . Whether they dress like the Kray twins or Deputy Dawg, it's important you don't allow yourself to be intimidated. But intimidation by your opponents is only one part of the relationship side of stress management.

When you play poker you will be suppressing a lot of emotion. (Or at least I hope you will!) This leads to unresolved relationships, which in turn can lead to grudges, resentments, animosity and even guilt if you feel bad about duping opponents out of their money. While it's possible to suppress these issues while you're bluffing they could cause leakage or even sabotage your playing decisions later in the game. Playing to get revenge is neither healthy nor clever.

Although you should conceal your emotions during the game it's important to recognise the danger of suppressed feelings. They can cause stress and then you can become a risky player. So it is not enough just to suppress them. You need to banish them altogether. Never take it personally. Let it drop – and by drop I do mean drop. Bad losers make bad players and so do guilty losers.

If you find your feelings towards other players are getting personal then salvage the situation with a couple of positive affirmations such as:

'Let it drop.'
'Life's too short.'
'Cancel and continue.'

DILEMMAS

It's easy to see the role of the dilemma in even the friendliest non-challenging game of poker. Your brain has multiple-choice decisions to make and the importance of those decisions increases with the size of the pot. It would be impossible to log the number of choices that are presented to you when you're dealt your cards, or the inner dialogues that go on as you evaluate those choices. The decisions you're making with each call are some of the most complex of your life and, although the decision-making process might be speedy, the mechanics involved are terribly advanced. Easy to see how this sort of dilemma can be stress-inducing.

Good fortune does little to lessen the burden. Consistently

losing can cause you to worry about the choices you're making. However, a run of wins can put you under pressure too, especially if you're not sure where your luck is coming from. It is a fact that in sport most teams feel more relaxed and confident if they're approaching a game as the underdog. Low expectations somehow make it easier to perform. It's the more experienced winning team that is under pressure to maintain its reputation.

Poker players most at risk are those who have been buoyed by early wins or a run of good luck but who are only just learning techniques. Instead of moving forward as they learn the game, they'll often be penned in by not wanting to change a winning formula. This means their fear makes them sustain a beginner's style of play and they never improve. Confusingly, an early winner may have to worsen their luck to learn to play better.

As well as physiological symptoms, there are three other areas that stress can affect that will be just as damaging to your poker techniques:

- Emotional effects.
- Cognitive effects.
- Behavioural effects.

Emotional effects

In many ways your ideal state will be one of 'I'm okay you're okay', which is the ultimate state of psychological confidence when your personal esteem levels are so high that you feel like a potential winner, but your respect for others is healthy as well, meaning you are wary but positive. This state is devoid of the arrogance that can blind you to potential danger or the need to put effort into your game, but it also lacks qualities like paranoia or resentment that can create bad calls based purely on negative emotions such as revenge.

The 'dread response' is especially dangerous to poker players as it sometimes feels like a kind of clairvoyance. When people suffer from 'stress dread' you'll often hear them saying they feel things are going to go wrong. Sometimes they think it's a bad idea to go out that day or that they are feeling unlucky. Their favourite catch phrase is, 'I knew that would happen.' They are continually expecting the worst and failing to register the best, even when it does happen. This negative tension is a false state yet it can affect the game you play. Although it's normally good to tune in to your gut reactions, this stress dread is deeply unreliable and best ignored.

Increased psychological tension is another side-effect of emotional stress. It exaggerates your negative emotions and makes it hard to be rational. When we get stressed we get niggly, petty, irritable, angry, upset – often for no reason at all. It goes without saying that you should never play poker in an emotional state. In body language terms, the best poker is played by someone so calm they are corpse-like. Negative emotional energy is not to be welcomed at the poker table if you want to be a winner. Nature has made our negative emotions very visible, just to scare other animals off when we're angry and about to fight. Suppressing them at times of heightened stress is just not feasible.

Increased physical tension can make you look like a coiled spring. This type of bodily pose would be better suited to sports like kick-boxing or wrestling where muscular prowess should be used as a boast. Letting your poker opponents know that you're ready to rip their heads off with your bare hands is of limited value and suggests you're capable of losing your cool and gambling recklessly.

Cognitive effects

The cognitive effects of stress are many and varied but all are less than helpful when it comes to poker. When you're over-stressed the odds are you'll also:

- Suffer from poor concentration, making it hard to remember other cards and how they were dealt.
- Be easily distracted, so that instead of monitoring your opponents' body language you're wondering how long before the crisps run out.
- Experience reduced short-term memory, so you have no idea whose turn it is next.
- Have difficulty making choices – always bad when you need to make rapid card decisions.

Behavioural effects

Disrupted sleep patterns leave you moody and below par when it comes to thinking straight. Even the loss of 20 per cent of your normal sleep time can have a noticeable effect on your poker performance. When you find it hard to sleep because of stress you may try to compensate by drinking or smoking more. Both of these will affect the sense of calm that is required for good poker thinking.

When these stress signals arrive you need to take action. Once the stress response kicks in and you try to work through it you can find it becomes a regular feature in your life. The longer you leave it the harder it is to manage. In the end the stress increases while the triggers decrease in size and importance. So while you may have got medium stress over a big game or tournament you find yourself getting extremely stressed over a 'friendly' game that doesn't matter.

BLAME BAGGAGE

The second effect of stress that you need to be wary of is the way you can begin to give away control over your life. You do this by blaming other people or events when you lose. This is called anger displacement. Your defeat should teach you some positive lessons about where you went wrong. This could help by ensuring you don't repeat those mistakes, like being too unsubtle when you bluffed.

The problem with self-criticism is that it's hard to accept. We need it but we don't like it. Instead of getting angry with ourselves we prefer to displace that anger and blame someone else. This is a natural reaction. It's your 'ego survival system' kicking in. It's never your fault. It was the poor deal, your opponent's odd smirk, the colour of the wallpaper or the fact you forgot to wear your lucky socks.

But can't this idea of blame just be a technique to keep your ego intact? If you don't think it's your fault, shouldn't that mean you avoid beating yourself up and thinking you're a bad player? Well actually, no. To play good poker you need to learn to move forwards. Blaming other people might help you feel better but it won't make you improve your game. It's important you recycle defeat into a search for success, not a search for a door marked 'Exit'. By accepting the blame you keep control of yourself. Control makes you less stressed, too. So drop the blame baggage.

HOW TO DE-STRESS

In a situation that is physically non-threatening, stress is all about mind over body.

Challenge your perceptions

Change your perceptions to change your state of mind. If you see your opponents as better players or intimidating personalities then start to imagine them in a less threatening light. Rise above the obvious. Create small ideas in your mind that will make them look ridiculous. Keep respect for their techniques but never be over-awed by their projected image.

Keep away from stressed players

If you see someone pacing or drumming before they go in to play walk away as quickly as possible. Stress is contagious.

Warm up

Warm up as part of your mental preparation. Go somewhere quiet and take a few moments (10 minutes would be ideal). Focus first on blanking your mind out, then on seeing the win using positive visualisations. Never spend your last few minutes before a game trying to remember moves or winning formulas. This is not the moment to learn new techniques.

Take exercise

The fight or flight instinct is intended to lead to physical activity. Trying to ignore that leads to fidgeting, pacing or internalised anxiety. Walking briskly, or even swimming or dancing before you play will help you to ease your muscle tension.

Keep it light

You need to lift your mood to decrease your stress levels. Find something that makes you laugh or cheers you up. Watch cartoons or a comedy show on TV or play classic comedy shows on your iPod. Listen to light but upbeat music, and avoid calming classical music as this can de-motivate or under-stimulate just before a big game.

Create a 'little book of madness'

This is a small notebook that you carry with you everywhere. Fill it with all your worries, frustrations, anger and negative thoughts. Getting your worries down on the printed page helps get them out of your head and is a great antidote to stress. Write while you think in a stream-of-consciousness way. Never censor, just chuck it down as it enters your head. This is ideal therapy to combat stress.

Sleep well

If you find tournament tension is disruptive to your sleep use positive techniques to try to regain your required sleep levels. For example:

- *Avoid coffee*: Don't drink caffeine beverages for about six hours before you go to bed – it stays in the bloodstream longer than you might think.
- *Create pre-sleep routines*: That way your body knows the right time to start shutting down for rest.
- *Avoid late-night baths or showers*: Don't have a hot bath just before you go to bed as this can stimulate rather than relax.

- *Keep your 'little book of madness' handy*: Have it by your bedside and use it during the night to offload any worries that may stop you getting to sleep.
- *Relax your mind*: Do nothing stimulating for an hour before going to bed. Wind down instead. Watch 'happy' TV programmes and be careful what you read in bed. Horror/action books, technical manuals or work should all be avoided.
- *Relax your jaw*: This muscle clenches when we get stressed and you can't sleep if your jaw is tight. Place the tip of your tongue in the middle of the roof of your mouth and push gently to make your jaw relax.
- *Relax your muscles*: Lie on your back with your eyes closed. Starting with your toes, flex and then relax every muscle in your body in turn until your whole body is eased of tension and you can drift off to sleep.
- *Try 'mental chewing gum'*: Pick a small and deeply unimportant mind task to work on. Maybe you could try to go through the alphabet finding a composer's or artist's name for each letter. Or you could try to come up with the plot of a new TV soap, game show or reality show. The blandness of the project is relaxing while the subject matter keeps more anxiety-inducing thoughts from keeping you awake.

SENSORY STRESS-BUSTERS

There are several quick-fix tips you can use to calm yourself before a major game. You'll have heard of stress-busters such as massage, aromatherapy and music therapy but you might have assumed that they work on anyone. In fact, their effectiveness will depend on your own very individual sensory stimulus, which often means that one sense will be more easily and powerfully affected than all the others. To discover your key stress 'trigger' sense do a short experiment:

- Find a comfortable chair in a darkened room that is quiet and set well away from any interruptions.
- Sit down and close your eyes.
- Get into the mental state for the visualisation techniques that we tried earlier in the book.
- Relax and empty your mind.
- Think back to a time in childhood when you were happy. Pick any moment and start to turn it around in your mind.
- Using your imagination, take yourself back to that time and place. Gradually relive the experience through your own child's eye.
- Do this for several minutes until the experience is over or you're starting to get distracted.
- Then open your eyes and think: What memory sense was the strongest? Did you enjoy the noises of music, sea, voices or seagulls? Or did you love the sights and colours of everything around you? Were you eating or tasting certain favourite foods, like ice-cream? Or did the smells of the food or scent of flowers make you happy? Did you feel warm sand between your toes or the fur of a pet you were stroking?
- By whittling down your sensory enjoyment you should be able to decide which sense experience was the strongest and most pleasurable. This will give you a guide to your preferred and most effective sense when you're doing quick techniques to create calm before a tournament or big game.

Calming colours

Colour therapy is a popular relaxation technique. You decide which colour has a positive effect. Keep in mind that different colours will have a different effect on your moods. Blues are the most calming so try focusing on blue tones, from pastel to violets. Yellow has an uplifting effect so choose this if you want to feel upbeat, optimistic and creative. Greens and browns create a mood of responsibility and honesty while reds excite the nervous system and may increase stress levels.

Stare at a patch of your chosen colour when you're feeling relaxed, then take a small piece of fabric in that colour with you when you play an important game. It takes 21 days to create or break a habit so the more you can connect this colour with a sense or relaxation prior to your game the more effective it will be when you get there.

Obviously you should avoid colour-staring in front of your opponents but you can do it in the toilet or even take a hankie, tie or scarf in the colour if you feel it will help. You could get a feeling of relaxation by looking at pictures. Some players flick through a glossy magazine just before a game to calm themselves.

Calming flavours

Like the associated colour technique, tastes can be calming. A good taste to use for instant calm is vanilla. This is said to link our memory with baby milk and therefore regresses you to a time when you felt safe and happy. Many players and performers swear by Bach's Rescue Remedy, a traditional relaxation product available from health food shops.

Calming aromas

Aromatherapy oils are famous for their ability to create calm. Lavender oil is the most popular for relaxation although for poker you might prefer to choose an essence that is both calming and uplifting. I use peppermint or lemon when I'm working. These create a feeling of well-being but not sleepiness.

Calming touch

If touch is your key sense then self-massage will help you relax. Touch slows the heart rate, which is a useful antidote to stress or anxiety. When I train business people I recommend they give themselves a DIY face or scalp massage at their desk. Of course at the poker table this would reveal your state of mind so do it out of sight.

Simply massage very lightly in gentle circles, using flattened fingertips. Work gently from just behind the ear, along your jaw line and into your hairline and around your forehead. Then, using very light pinching movements, work your way along your eyebrows to the bridge of your nose.

A foot workout is also invigorating but calming. Take off your shoes and spread your toes wide, keeping your feet on the floor. Pretend you're picking something up from the floor with your feet, clenching and unclenching your toes. Now lift your feet slightly and circle them from the ankle, three times clockwise, and three times anticlockwise.

Another tactile technique is the 'magic stress touch'. Using the 21-days-to-create-or-kick-a-habit theory you can pick a similar 'touch' gesture that will create calm when you use it under pressure. Try a simple movement such as rubbing the top of your thumb or your earlobe or massaging the heel of your hand. Do it for 21 days when you're already feeling secure and relaxed, especially when you're getting off to sleep. Then do it when you're tense, stressed or anxious and you'll find it calms you down.

Calming sounds

You can learn to self-calm using music or even voices. You probably find music soothing already. So pinpoint exactly what type of music puts you in what type of mood. Classical will usually be calming but might make you feel sleepy too. Baroque is the best thinking music, although if you connect it with 'Musak' then you could find it annoys rather than lifts.

Be imaginative but be reflective. What songs cheer you up/motivate you/make you feel braver/calmer/stronger? The good thing about music is that you can be prescriptive, choosing the right music for the right mood. Or you might want to try voices instead. If you could hear your parents' muffled voices as you went off to sleep as a child you might find the sound soothing now. Several relaxation tapes feature the sound of an expert talking on top of the music. Or you could try talking books for the voices rather than the plots. If Harry Potter does it for you *en route* to a game then get it onto your headphones.

7

YOUR POKER FACE IN PLACE

Your body language behaviour will form a 'ripple effect' that can – and probably will – influence your opponents' gambling decisions. Even a small movement from you could tilt the balance dramatically. By working on your poker face and performance techniques you can work the game in your own favour.

RIPPLE EFFECT

We mentioned the 'affecting factors' in Chapter 4. Now it's time to study them in detail. Most of this ripple effect caused by the 'affecting factors' is subconscious, so your opponents won't even know how they have been affected. Subtlety is always a stronger tool than exaggeration.

For example, when opponents are deciding on a call they have only a limited amount of time to make their decision. If, during the pause, you make a small throat-clearing noise or shift very slightly in your seat, this could put subliminal pressure on them to hurry up. This action might apply a slight pressure or a strong pressure, depending on their upbringing and social conscience.

Deadlines activate the brain but pressure agitates it. This will affect their thinking processes, making them more impulsive and less logical. There's no guarantee this will work in your favour but you can assume that you've made your opponent's thinking less orderly and act on that, especially if you've already noticed how he or she responds when placed under pressure.

PLAY FOR TODAY

But that's the smaller movements. What about a performed bluff? Acting makes the game richer and more exciting. When you bluff, the ripple effect increases dramatically, especially if your opponents guess you might be bluffing. Whatever you do will have an effect on their game. Bluffing will change the way they play. Therefore it's true to say that bluffing always works. It won't guarantee that you win but it will affect your opponents' strategies in one way or another. It places more power in your hands. You can change their game. It's up to you to work out how.

Start with friends or family

You might think that playing with people you know and love is an easy way to start. Where's the pressure in that? You might even see it as an exercise in bonding. Well, in 'poker face' terms, close relatives and friends are your worst nightmare. It might be stating the obvious but never forget *they know you well* and so will be able to tell when you're bluffing. They know your 'normal' behaviour patterns and so they will spot any deviations a mile away.

The worst of the bunch is your mother. She is able to read your non-verbal signals in a very spooky and uncanny way. Remember, she was the one who could tell what you were saying before you could speak. When you were a baby, she would monitor your every move and expression and announce whether you were hungry, sick or needed your nappy changing. Now she is able to monitor the state of your health from the tone of your voice during a transatlantic phone call. If you send her a one-line text she'll be able to tell that your marriage is on the skids, so imagine her rate of accuracy in reading you when you're sitting face-to-face across a card table.

Then there's your partner. He or she will have a marginally less accurate hit rate than your mother but has seen you lie on numerous occasions and so knows the form well. Having had experience of scanning your face for signals that you're having an affair or forgot to set the video for the final of *Big Brother*, spotting your subtle give-aways or leakage signals is child's play.

Work colleagues have a similar skill. They've observed all your lies from the 'sickie' excuse to the 'e-mail-must-have-got-lost-I-know-I-sent-it' act. They believed none of your guff then and will believe none of it when you try to bluff over your hand.

BLUFFING WITH CLOTHING

Bluffing can easily become costume drama. In Part Two I analyse what your opponents' clothing can tell you about their style of play. But you might feel like making clothing part of your bluff, too, dressing in a way that implies characteristics you don't have. There are many ways to do this, of course, depending on the effect you want to create. You might dress to dazzle or delude, confuse or confound. It all depends on your persona. As an example, you could dress to fool your opponents into a false sense of security – what I call the 'Columbo effect'.

The Columbo effect

We've all seen the TV series *Columbo*, either first time round or repeats. This long-running saga featured a brilliant and meticulously analytical detective who was able to fool his murder suspects into making mistakes by the very simple device of wearing a scruffy overcoat and acting the bumbling fool. As Columbo ambled around saying and doing stupid things, the highly educated suspect (usually clad in a cravat) would, in turn, become amused, patronising, irritated and finally horrified when Columbo revealed himself to be a skilful and cunning opponent.

Dumbing down can be a hugely effective device for winning the odd game of poker but keep in mind that your opponents will have sussed you after a couple of games. The Columbo technique also relies on you playing people who've never met you before. Unless you want to convince friends or family that you have suddenly lost your dress sense along with your marbles, it's unlikely they'll be suckered in by an acute attack of dopeyness if you're normally known to be smart and astute.

Older people will find it easier to 'pull off a Columbo' than younger players. The young have little concept of the oscillations of the brain after the age of 50 and so sudden attacks of stupidity or forgetfulness will be readily accepted. One or two bouts of asking if anyone's seen your glasses when you're quite clearly wearing them on top of your head will be more than adequate to convince them that you're easy meat at the poker table. Here are a few tips to make it work:

- When the winning pot is pushed towards you, look shocked and mortified.
- Say, 'I won again? How? I don't believe it!'
- Apologise to the other players.

- Offer to give some money back.
- As with every bluff, keep in mind that subtlety is king. Success should never spur you on to an even more over-the-top performance.

A warning

Sometimes these ploys not only fool your opponents, they fool your own brain, too. If you dress scruffily and act a bit dim, be careful you don't get what you wish for. The body is highly receptive to others' subliminal signals but the reverse can be true too. Be careful that a dumbed-down routine doesn't become method acting and fool your subconscious. If you play stupid you could easily start to act stupid. It's hard to adopt a bumbling persona without your brain joining in the act.

YOUR PLAYER PERSONALITY

'Player personality' is often as much a surprise to the gambler as it is to his or her opponents. Some people had no idea they had a ruthless streak until they sat down with their first hand. Others find the opposite and start letting people win because they feel sorry for them. This ruthlessness and need to win at whatever cost might not surface during normal life.

I once played 'friendly' cards with a couple I had known for years and during the evening we all discovered to our surprise, then shock and finally horror that the wife – one of the nicest, kindest people you'd ever want to meet – was playing cards in a way that would have made a riverboat gambler blush. She systematically shafted everyone around the table, including her loyal and adoring husband, her best friend (me) and her young son, for whom her devotion knew no bounds. After 30 minutes it became clear she would have happily ripped off Mother Teresa and a cartload of sickly and needy orphans if only they'd pitched up and asked to be dealt a hand.

Niceness in the real world is no guide to poker behaviour, then, so jettison any pre-conceived thoughts about personality patterns before you sit down to play with people you know. Assume any or all of them are capable of latent criminal behaviour and work backwards from that thought.

Remember that your main aim as a wannabe winner is to confuse: to take behaviours they know and spin them in every direction. Be constantly on the move, gullible one minute, open and honest the next and as devious as a character off *Showboat* straight after. Bluff, double-bluff and treble-bluff. But never remain becalmed.

BLUFFING YOUR FAMILY

Try to remember that when it comes to bluffing your nearest and dearest you're your own worst enemy. You'll only fail if you let yourself down. So how and why might this happen?

Guilt

Guilt will inhibit your ability to modulate your non-verbal signals. Deep down inside every one of us there is a small child that wants to be good. That child will feel pressure to be honest with the people it knows best. In part, this is because of survival. Animals need teams to survive the longest as numbers equal strength. The easiest team to form is a family. When you try to bluff or compete with members of your own family your subconscious will feel you're alienating yourself from your own personal team.

The moral brain

It's hard to play logically when your moral brain keeps trying to take over. When you look at your opponents, one part of your brain will be working out how to beat them while the other starts to imagine how they'll feel when they get trounced, how losing the pot will affect their finances and how they'll take being bluffed by a family member or close friend. This moral movement is destructive to your game.

Denial gestures

The pressure caused by guilt or morality can emerge in the form of 'denial gestures'. These are usually small and even fleeting but nearly always perceptible to the naked eye, when your body decides to reveal your true feelings in their most negative form. An example I see all the time is when I'm training people to do a sales pitch. I call this the 'lemming moment' – when salespeople are unsure how to fill the small pause that occurs when they've finished speaking.

Suddenly all the guilt and insecurity bubbles to the surface in the form of a small shrug of the shoulders, twitch of the mouth, quirky smile, eye roll or rapid flapping of the hands. Sometimes the hands are clasped in front of the body and both feet will roll outward in a childish pose that looks unsophisticated even on a five- year-old. This is a subliminal cry for reassurance. Despite the fact that they've been trying to sell something they have a deep-rooted desire to be honest in order to win friends and influence people. It's the child within making a desperate break for freedom, like Steve McQueen on his motorbike in *The Great Escape*.

Mirroring

By mirroring or mimicking someone else's body language, we get a clearer understanding of their thoughts and feelings. This is a natural process between friends, but you can simulate it with regular poker opponents. By mimicking their movements in private you'll gain a greater insight into their thoughts and feelings.

The poker face mask

If your hand is good and you want to prevent the other players from folding early you'll need to mask your excitement and positive anticipation. 'Over-masking' by applying a contradictory expression might confuse your opponents but the natural outcome would be for you to fold and this is what they'll expect. Hence the introduction of the poker face. If you have a weak hand and want to give the appearance of holding a strong one in an attempt to lure your opponents into thinking they can beat you, it might sound logical to apply a mask of unease or frustration. But if your mask is too obvious your opponents will either think you're a beginner or a fool or guess you're masking and must therefore have a good hand.

Experienced poker players often overcome this dilemma by keeping the poker face in place throughout the game, or they will be over-animated, chatting and using exaggerated gestures in an effort to disguise the truth. In many ways this is like hiding a tree in a forest. Both techniques can intimidate other players.

THE GREAT GIVE-AWAYS

It's relatively easy to create a smile-lie. But replicating distress, upset, frustration or misery is deeply difficult. A child who falls over will play-act distress to get attention and comfort. But the role-play was triggered by the event, which was genuine, even if the distress was exaggerated. Playing poker is different. Play-acting your response to a bad hand when you're gazing at a winner will test your dramatic powers to the full. Remember that to perform a lie we must first experience the real emotion, which could be exaltation if the hand is a good one. Then we have to suppress that truth and create the lie. Two of the key facial muscles needed to create a smile are in regular use but the muscles needed to manufacture a false expression of distress are not. It's virtually impossible to look upset when you're actually quite happy.

Play-acting the double-bluff should be easier. This is where we indicate the truth in a way that suggests we're lying. For example, in a verbal version of this ploy, a woman might ask her husband if he's having an affair. He has three options; the third is the double-bluff:

1. Tell the truth as the truth: 'Yes, I've been seeing her for months.'
2. Tell a lie: 'No, of course I'm not.'
3. Tell the truth as a lie: 'Of course. I have affairs with all my colleagues.'

LEAKAGE

It is important to mask your happiness at that moment when your eyes hit the cards and send a message to your brain that you're primed to win the pot. Similarly, you need to hide the signs that say you have little to work with and are flying by the seat of your pants. Either way, it is important to know the give-aways that reveal the true state of your hand.

Your face is the central focus and screen for all your feelings and emotions, yet the emotions you display to others are rarely seen by yourself. The face you see when you look in the mirror is a bland mask. In many ways it's like the screensaver on your PC, something that appears when you're in repose. When you play poker, that bland mask can easily slip, unless you consciously hold it in place. Your words are controlled and selected by your brain, but facial expressions are usually triggered by your emotions. We have little real idea how our faces look when we're speaking to others.

For example, excessive or increased head movement could easily contradict your poker face or performed bluff. Your head tends to dance in time with your thoughts rather than your words and is a strong indicator of your inner feelings. Avoid head tilts or nodding unless using them as part of a performed bluff.

Tiny involuntary facial movements, called micro-gestures, might occur as you attempt a poker face or bluff. Sometimes a small muscle will work away in your jaw when you are under pressure, or there might be a barely perceptible tightening of your lips. These movements send out a clear signal to opponents. Use relaxation exercises to suppress muscle tension in the face. Asymmetrical expressions, such as a lop-sided grin, are also give-aways, creating the impression of being literally 'two-faced'. All parts of the face give away their own unique clues.

Your eyes

The eyes signal emotion in four different ways:

- *Direction of gaze*: You need to decide on your levels of eye contact and direction of gaze. If you're trying to bluff, avoid over-stating your eye contact. A solid stare is unnatural and will tell your opponent you're bluffing. If you look upward and to one side you could reveal whether you're genuinely calculating play or deciding whether to bluff so try to keep your eyes cast down and to the middle when you do look away. This is the most regular and neutral eye direction.

- *Eye shape*: The muscles around the eye can soften the expression or harden into a stare. When we are relaxed these muscles are soft. But tension may make your eye muscles go rigid. So try to create a softened eye expression to feign calm. Imagine you're looking at someone or something you really like and this should create a relaxed eye shape.

- *Pupil size*: The pupils widen (dilate) when you're happy or emotional about what you see. It's an involuntary response and impossible to prevent. If you're bluffing, avoid looking straight from your cards into your opponents' eyes as they might spot the dilation, or lack of it, and tell if you have a very strong hand or a very weak one.

- *Blink rate*: The number of times you blink per minute increases when under emotional pressure, such as anger or anxiety. The normal blink rate is about 20 per minute but can increase to as much as 100 per minute. To be aware of your blinking might seem like a tall order but it is a strong subliminal give-away, especially if the increase is sporadic. Ideally, you need to try to stick to the normal 20-per-minute rate – but I don't expect you to practise with a stop-watch.

Your nose

It *will* grow, you know. It wasn't just Pinocchio. According to scientists at the University of Illinois with too much time on their hands, the pressure to lie makes the heart pump faster and causes the capillaries in the nose to expand. This makes the hairs inside the nose stand up and, in turn, creates the desire to touch or scratch your nose. If you want to bluff you could use this classic 'lie' gesture and perform it subtly to mislead. But if you're single-bluffing and telling opponents you have a strong/weak hand your nose-touch gesture could suggest you're being deceptive. So keep the hands away from the face unless it's part of your planned performance.

Your breathing

When under pressure your breathing will become more frequent and more shallow. Breathing exercises and warm-ups are essential to avoid this give-away. A sharp intake or puff of air as you see your cards is something else you'll need to prepare for or it will have occurred before you realise it. Holding your breath is not an option as you'll let everyone know you're bluffing. The best plan is to let your breath out just before the cards are dealt. This relaxes the body and allows tension to escape before a response is called for and analysed. It will also help you control your breathing, which would otherwise be spontaneous and therefore uncontrollable.

Your voice

The voice is directly affected by your emotions. The pitch of your voice may change when you bluff. Excitement, anxiety, anger or tension can all have an effect. Sometimes the lie might make you feel as though you're being throttled and this makes it hard to drop to your normal pitch and tone. But try to hold your voice steady when your mouth dries and your vocal cords contract. The stress of a lie can also lead to breathlessness (see page 110).

Nervousness about the lie might make you forget the script. People who are caught on the hop will often have to stall for time to allow them to fast-track the process of thinking the truth, suppressing it and creating the lie. Apprehension can also change the length of your pauses or alter the way you speak, leading to pauses at the start of a key point, or use of verbal fillers like 'um . . . ' or 'er . . .' or short-burst pauses at frequent intervals that make your speech sound staccato or elongated.

Long pauses before answering, or no pauses at all, will also alert your opponents. The first might seem as though you're manufacturing the bluff and stalling for time while you prepare to deliver it. The second might look too speedy. Like the unblinking stare, this is overdoing things and will stink of a bluff.

Stammering can imply nervousness prompted by anxiety. If you stammer under pressure, remember to pace your speech and never rush. If you start to trip over your words you'll need to take a pause to avoid setting off a chain of stammering. If you're thinking of performing a stammer as part of a bluff, think again. It's normally involuntary, like a sneeze, so it can be very hard to replicate and sound natural.

Your smile

People often apply a smile of 'delight' when losing to an opponent or signal friendship to a customer who's being difficult. A smile is by far the easiest mask to slip on as it's the one we use the most in everyday transactions. We slap on a smile when we're only a few months old and we use it to manipulate bonding and protective instincts in adults.

Smiling is a social signal of greeting that implies lack of intent to fight or cause damage. In many ways it's a reassurance gesture. When humans get into the company of other humans we throw a smile out and if we get a smile in return we feel mildly relieved and safe. Even in a relatively non-threatening scenario like the office we feel threatened when a smile of greeting fails to get a matching response. Our response is often to feel anger or fear and a desire to fight or flee.

Muscle tension caused by stress can make it difficult to talk or smile normally. You may also feel compelled to cover your mouth when you bluff, as though embarrassed by your own lie. In practice, you won't usually cover the mouth, but it is common to make light touching movements, such as placing a finger on the lips or tapping the mouth, which betrays the unconscious desire to hide the lie.

A genuine smile requires four key facial muscles but a fake smile uses only two. A smile starts in the left brain, which sends signals to the right side of the face. The right brain signals to the left side of the mouth. A genuine smile though will involve the muscles of the eye as well. In fact, the smile is the most popular body language lie and there are several obvious give-aways that will show when your best poker smile is an act:

- A false smile rarely reaches the eyes.
- A fake smile is often lop-sided.
- The effort required will often produce a smile that is too large, called the 'stretched social smile'.
- The teeth are often clenched behind the false smile.
- When we fake it we often smile too soon, before the punch-line.

- The fake smile may be too fleeting, appearing from nowhere and disappearing just as quickly. This is called the 'lightning smile'.

So if you want to create a bluff of genuine-looking pleasure, make sure your smile is even and that it shows in the eyes too.

Your hands

We tend to focus on words and facial expressions and often let the hands, feet and posture look after themselves, which is a huge mistake when you're trying to bluff. This is probably because we tend to disregard the rest of the body and misjudge its importance when making up a lie. In fact, your body is much easier to control and lie with than your face. For one thing, you can see most of it, and for another, it's not operated directly by the emotions. So why is it an easy target for leakage then?

The language of the hands is difficult to control. They can be signalling for help without you realising it. If you make too many hand gestures it will look like showmanship. Move your hands too little and you'll look as though you're repressing your gestures and therefore bluffing. Use the wrong gestures that signal the opposite messages to your words and they'll know you're executing a bluff. This is called 'incongruent signalling'. But overdo the right gestures and you'll look 'over-congruent', meaning you'll be revealing your bluff via your overacting.

When you lie you tend to cut down on all hand movement or exaggerate it. Monitor your own normal hand movements and replicate them under pressure or cut right down from arrival to the end of the game. Avoid becoming more animated in breaks.

Hand-to-face touching will always signal stress or distress. Unless this is a practised bluff keep your hands away from your face at all times.

Your feet

Research suggests that when people are lying they tend to have more 'leakage' signals in the lower half of their body. Feet like to keep up their own unspoken dialogue, tapping, twitching or tucking themselves away underneath the table. You might think your feet are invisible under the table but if you're bluffing it's good to do a whole-body bluff so get them in on the act.

Body noises

Did you realise you make a lot of noise? Breathing, sniffing, clearing your throat, swallowing and tapping. Not to mention stomach rumbling. All of these noises will increase when you are under pressure.

Thinking pause

You need to make sure your 'thinking signals' don't give your hand away. If you pause to think only when your hand is mediocre then that will become your personal piece of 'leakage' and you will be unmasked by perceptive opponents. You'll need to use a sham move now and again, spending more thinking time over a winning hand just to confuse your opponents. When you do this, though, please don't overact. Vary the pace of your thinking and pauses. Don't let them drag on too long or you could become annoying. Pick one 'thinking gesture' and use it subtly.

Continue to use it when you are genuinely thinking. Remember, continuity is vital.

Sham-thinking

If you choose to employ 'sham' thinking, be clear in your mind why you're doing this. If genuine, it usually means your hand is neither the best nor the worst. So, your thinking bluff will be performed for two main reasons:

- To give the impression that you have a mediocre hand when you have a good one, or
- To destabilise your opponents if you feel they're looking for patterns in your behaviour. If you always play straight then the minute you pause to think they can comfortably assume you have a mediocre hand. You'll need to spend thinking time on a good or even excellent hand, to prevent this happening.

If you decide to use this bluff it would be better to opt for one signal of thinking rather than going through the whole Royal Shakespeare Company experience. This is a poker table, not the Royal Court. Avoid face-tapping, frowning, going 'hmm' or sucking air through puckered lips.

Often it's easy to start subtly but then be tempted to build up your performance once you feel it's going well. You may think that as you have the attention of your audience, why not milk it for all it's worth? Well, for one reason, only very bad liars overact. Remember the dreaded 'over-congruent signalling'. The more you add to your act the more your opponents will spot that you're bluffing.

You could sit back in your chair, you could take in a longer breath, you could place a finger lightly over your lips, you could adopt a small frown. But don't do all of these or even go for the ceiling stare or 'hmm'. What you're attempting to replicate is a polite but unguarded signal of daily etiquette to apologise for holding other people up.

Never take your mini-drama to the next step – the faux-dither. Over-confidence is the enemy of subtlety and this is no place for showboating. Scrunching your face up, going 'er . . .' or stretching your mouth into a suppressed smile are banned on the grounds of overacting.

Peeking bluff

This is where you peek at your cards to signal, say, uncertainty. If you feel this is a useful signal to send out then use it. But if you have a good hand you'll need to wipe your face of all expression of pleasure. Before you mock-peek, your face must register mild concern rather than suppressed glee. So you'll have to avoid any signs that indicate happiness, such as:

- *Face-softening*: Your face tends to smooth out and the expression will soften when you see something you like.
- *Pupil dilation*: Again, this is a pleasure give-away.
- *Smirking*: Avoid even the smallest micro-gesture suggestion of a smile.
- *Face-covering*: Any attempt to hide your true expression is a give-away.
- *Smarty-pants eye expression*: It's a glance that tries very hard to be deadpan but misses by a mile. It's human nature to crow via our body language when we've done something clever even if we are verbally modest at the same time.

- *Over-egged look of gloom*: You might look a little deadpan if you were indeed peeking at a bad hand but mournful eyes and an expression of deep regret will show you're just acting.

So now you've taken control of your own body language it's time to move on and take a look at your opponents'. Are they bluffing or not? Should you believe what your eyes are telling you or go with your gut reactions?

In Part Two I'm going to help you overcome your upbringing and turn into a perceptive starer. We'll be looking at all your opponents' bluffs and lies and keeping track of their leakage and performances. Forget tricks, tells and wizardry; you'll be rediscovering skills of reading others that you were born with and discovering how to use them to win at poker.

To end Part One, here's John Duthie's 'best tip' for personal poker success:

'To be constantly aware of how you behave when you have a strong hand and try to simulate this when you don't. You have to firmly believe that you have the best hand. Imagine the cards that you want to make your opponent believe you are holding and maintain that image at the front of your mind until they fold. If they call your bluff then analyse the hand afterwards and see if there was any specific point where you let your guard down and try never to do this again. It isn't easy and the larger the bets the more difficult it becomes.'

PART TWO: UNMASKING THE BLUFFER

8

HOW TO STARE

Before you can begin to look for clues about your opponents' hands you need to get used to being watchful. This chapter gives you hints and tips about increasing your skills of visual perception. Can you tell when someone is lying or bluffing just by looking at them? The easy answer is 'yes'. So the next question is, why do criminal cases go to trial when the guilty or not guilty verdict could be sussed out by a lie expert? The answer is that the way someone moves or talks when they lie will give clues rather than a definitive answer. When you judge someone by looking at them you are sifting through what is virtually signal overload, watching their eyes, face, posture, gestures and movement alongside their words and vocal tone.

When you assess someone in a natural, 'animal' way you look for what are called 'cluster signals'. Your eyes assimilate many different messages, weigh one up against the other and emerge with an overall response. This is why looking at a single movement and attaching thoughts and feelings to that one gesture alone is ridiculous. In many ways it's like working out a speaker's meaning from a single word they utter. To know what that word means you have to see it in the context of a sentence. To understand a gesture you have to see it in relation to all the other gestures being performed at the same time.

For instance, what would you think if someone pointed at you? The finger point is a signal of aggression so you could feel you were under attack. But before you responded you'd check out the eye expression, posture and general demeanour of the pointer. If they were smiling or laughing you'd probably accept the point was low aggression. If the pointer was frowning or shaking their head you might get ready to run.

THE OTHELLO ERROR

Reading other people's lies or bluffs is a complex skill but that should never put you off. What you must learn to do is make a judgement based on a balance of incoming information. Cutting corners isn't cheating but it will help you lose an awful amount of money if you're betting on one gesture or look. If you only look at one gesture or movement to read a person's thoughts, you're very likely to fall foul of what psychologists call 'The Othello Error'.

Othello believed his wife Desdemona's distress was prompted by guilt at being questioned over an affair, but it was actually agitation prompted by fear of being murdered by him. Any one word we use when we speak can have several meanings. It's only when it's put into the context of a sentence that you start to understand it.

Take the word 'jelly', for instance. This word means different things to different people. You may have visualised a big wobbly dessert. Or perhaps a smaller fruit pastille. To some people, jellies mean small shots of alcohol encased in a sweet, while to others they are a plastic beach shoe. In some parts of the North a jelly is a condom.

The good news is that your brain is able to cope with all this influx of information. The bad news is that it isn't guaranteed to come up with an accurate interpretation. The other piece of good news is that liars rarely manage to pull off a full-body lie. Most people are aware of the parts of their appearance that they believe *you* will be most aware of when they prepare to lie. We all think about the words we use, for instance, and most of us would consider the expression on our face. But very often the effort of the charade is too exhausting to involve any other body parts. So hands and feet, for example, will often provide leakage signals, giving the game away.

Much of your ability to read other people and anticipate their intentions is instinctive. In crisis situations, we might even act on received signals about another person before our conscious brain has worked out what those signals were. When you sit on a train, your brain is extra-alert for signs of danger from your fellow passengers. You might move carriage if you felt something was wrong. This response could well occur before your conscious brain had worked out what was actually wrong and what you thought the other passenger might do. The fear response could be real. You could be sweating and shaking but all based on the speediest of signal-reading that you might put down to 'a feeling' or 'gut-reaction'.

Sadly, if we re-analyse or add consciousness to the process it will slow it down. When a goalie waits for a penalty he or she will have to make several quick-fire decisions based on lightning subconscious signals. If the conscious brain starts to butt in and examine each stage of the process then the whole system trips up and the ball is in the back of the net before the goalie has even moved.

This slowing down can be negative but in learning to play poker you'll have enough time to train your conscious mind to butt in for a swift re-examination of the facts and then get it to butt out so that your decisions can be speedy again.

This learning process is a lot like learning to drive. You learn consciously, slowly and possibly painfully and then pack the skill away in your subconscious. To do this you practise until you get the hang of it.

If you now took an advanced driver's course you would need to regurgitate your subconscious knowledge. This would make your driving slower and less professional, for a time. But what you are actually doing is re-learning and re-examining existing skills in order to improve them. Once you'd done that you'd be able to stuff them back into what's called 'muscle memory' and get back up to your original speed again.

ACTIVE LISTENING

The first skill of reading other people's body language signals is having the ability to listen. When you want to access someone's thoughts you need to do what's called 'active listening' which is a whole world away from the passive kind.

The vast majority of our daily communications come under the heading of 'dead communication'. Whether it is spoken, written, e-mailed, posted, stuck on notice boards or plastered on TV, it is outgoing communication only. There is no recipient. People might hear, read or watch what's said but it fails to penetrate those parts of the brain known as 'memory', 'meaning' or 'action'.

Much of what you hear people say goes in one ear and out the other without making much impact *en route*. We suffer from information overload in modern life, with our brain providing its own spam filter, disregarding and rejecting anything it sees as low priority or on a 'need to know' basis only.

This is called 'passive listening'. The best way to describe 'passive listening' is to imagine the scene in most homes on a weekday evening. One partner walks in from work and the first question is, 'How was your day?' This is, by and large, a verbal ritual that is rarely followed by prolonged bouts of 'active listening'. What usually happens next is that the speaker begins a litany of workplace problems and gripes while the listener goes about their business making sympathetic noises during any dramatic pauses. During this type of 'passive listening' the words are heard but the emotional meaning is ignored. Our listening ability makes us able to understand a million subtleties in any communication but often we're too busy or just too bored to bother with all the incoming mail.

By contrast, 'active listening' means listening to all the subtleties of a received communication. To do this you need to balance the words against the speaker's vocal tone and their non-verbal signals, that is, body language. This is easier than it sounds. Imagine your son or daughter comes home and enters the room quietly, head down. You ask if they're okay and they mumble an affirmative before running upstairs and slamming the bedroom door. Would you believe the 'yes' and walk off humming happily to yourself or would you recognise something was wrong and try to work out what it was?

We most often use 'active listening' in crisis situations. Playing poker can be described as a crisis situation. You may have your own money on the table and the risk is you'll lose it. Or you might be playing for popcorn or Smarties and you stand to lose face. Either way you need to win. So you'll need to employ the skills of 'active listening', which means using your ears *and* eyes. You are hearing what the other person is saying while evaluating it against their visual signals. This means picking out the 'incongruent signals' – i.e. those times when the words don't match up with the visual signals – and the 'over-congruent signals' – when the signals match but seem to be exaggerated.

Keep this thought in mind when you're trying to work out whether poker opponents are bluffing. Unless they've perfected the art of the poker bluff, their body language will probably be:

- *Underperformed*: Their body is unnaturally still, trying to give nothing away.
- *Incongruent*: Some gestures will signal one thing but other signals appear to conflict, causing body language 'leakage'.
- *Over-congruent*: All their signals are in agreement but they appear over-emphasised.

STARING

'Active watching and listening' is easy – you do it all the time. Half the time you don't even know you're doing it, that's how easy it is. But exactly who are you normally watching and listening to? Who do you attend to closely enough to discover all those hidden depths to their communication?

Your partner?
Colleagues at work?
Your boss?
Strangers on the train?
People in the pub?

If you said 'yes' to the first option it's likely you're in the early stages of a relationship. Lovers use active watching and listening techniques to fast-track empathy and rapport with their partner. Which is why when you see a couple sitting face-to-face in a bar or restaurant gazing into one another's eyes you can bet they're either within the first two years of the relationship or they're both married – but to other people – and having an affair. Intense face-watching and body-reading is rife through this stage as we try to reach inside our partner's brain to check they love us as much as we love them.

If you answered 'yes' to any or all of the other options you're probably a regular visitor to the Accident & Emergency department. Why? Because staring at people who are not in love with you makes them wary and even aggressive. Stranger-staring is an especially risky sport, which is why the one phrase that always signals the start of a pub punch-up is 'Who're you looking at?'

The only other people we are allowed to watch for fun and/or deeper understanding are those we see on our TV screens every night. Which is why for many people *Big Brother* housemates feel more like acquaintances and friends than the real McCoy.

In the animal world, staring is a sign of attraction or aggression. Which means you're probably not as good at staring as you should be or want to be. Keep in mind though that it wasn't always so. Up until the age of two you were a magnificent starer. When you were born you had no ability to survive without assistance and so as soon as your eyes focused you were happily monitoring and reading people from their various facial expressions, many of which you would mimic in a desperate attempt to bond and be nurtured.

As you became mobile you quickly started developing this wonderful skill of people-reading until the day came when you were told by a parent that 'It's rude to stare.' Confusing or what? The one core skill that's vital to your survival and you're told that it breaches the rules of social etiquette. So you spent the rest of your life trying to suss people out via surreptitious glances and peripheral vision.

When you meet someone you'd like to mate with you probably find you have a huge desire to look away quickly because your feelings of attraction make you socially embarrassed. This could be the person you'll be sleeping with, maybe for the rest of your life, and yet you can only glance at them for a fraction of a second at a time. Imagine if the same social body language rule applied to buying a car or a house, peeking at it before deciding to make the purchase!

So it's your parents' fault that you're a lousy people reader. As a result of this restriction on staring you probably feel you're not very good at telling what people are thinking or unmasking liars. The good news is you're probably a whole lot better than you think. What you've been describing as 'gut reaction' when you get a feeling about someone or something they are saying is very probably more scientific than you realise. Remember that when you meet someone for the first time those initial impressions are based on a computer-like assimilation of their non-verbal signals.

The only reason you're inaccurate is if you apply stereotype and assumption to the process. By this I mean you assume someone must be lying because they keep covering their mouth, when in reality it's because they wear a brace on their teeth. Or you think someone's being negative because they keep folding their arms when in fact it's because the room is too cold. We're going to create a much more potent and effective brew by employing logic and analysis alongside your intuition.

HOW TO STARE

Stare-master

But first you need to do away with the inhibitions of a lifetime and start staring. If you go all coy around a poker table you do yourself no favours at all. To learn to read people you first have to look. Fortunately you have access to a very powerful stare-arena in the comfort of your own living room, in the shape of your TV.

The deluge of reality TV has provided you with the best stare work-out tool you could have. These shows turn your TV into a one-way mirror, giving you access to total strangers as they love, fight, lie and compete. More importantly, these people can be studied by you *without prejudice*. You have no ulterior motive for the decisions you make about their behaviour and their personality. In psychology terms you're making a 'cold call'. Unlike real-life assessments you're not going to befriend them, bed them or hire them.

And this makes TV assessments the closest you'll get to reading your opponents in a poker game. You can be emotionally removed and therefore a much more accurate analyst. In reality TV, the housemates or competitors are all aware of your scrutiny and trying to impress you favourably so that you'll vote for them and they'll win the series. To do this they try to bluff the viewer, adopting a range of winning personality techniques that they think will score them points. Reality viewers like to look behind the performance, though, just as you'll be doing with your opponents in poker.

Another way to hone your lie-detecting skills is to seek out any keynote TV interviews where emotions are on show. You know the type of thing. A royal tries to make a pitch to the public or a politician attempts to prove that they're innocent of financial wrongdoing. This type of interview normally involves close-up camera work and this is always rich pickings for any students of body language, particularly for poker players who want to learn how to sniff out the lie.

PEOPLE-WATCHING EXERCISES

Here are some exercises to try to help you hone your people-watching skills.

Exercise 1
Look through the pages of a one-week TV guide. Pick out all the programmes that involve reality TV, such as *Big Brother*. Select a good mix to record.

- Watch the recordings with a pen and paper to hand.
- Watch them first 'as live', viewing in your normal style, using your normal amount of attention or perception.
- When the programme is over write down any observations about the characters you have just seen, including their personality, mood, interaction with others and relationship with others.

Now ask yourself the following 10 questions:

1.   Did they look comfortable or uncomfortable?
2.   Did they appear open or do you think they have something to hide?
3.   Did they look nervous or anxious?
4.   Did they seem to mean what they said?
5.   Did they like the interviewer/other people?
6.   Were they aggressive or passive?
7.   Did they look stressed?
8.   Were there any moments when their anxiety increased?

9. Did they use manipulative techniques like flirting or childishness?
10. Did they do anything to try to dominate the space or other people?

Exercise 2

Position yourself in a 'safe' place in public where you can watch people without looking like a pervert.

- Monitor a couple or small group of people who are involved in a verbal or non-verbal transaction.
- Write down your first impressions. For example, do they look like tourists, friends, a couple, strangers? (Perhaps one has stopped to ask directions, one is in charge and looks like the parent, or they look as though they're in love.)
- Then progress to the second stage of perception. Seek out more information. What are the status signals of the entire group?
- Are they close friends or merely acquaintances? Do the emotional ties look even?
- Who is the most animated?
- What type of gestures do they use as they talk?
- Do their gestures look 'congruent'? In other words, do all their signals appear to be in harmony or are they sending out conflicting messages?
- What micro-gestures do you notice? In other words, can you spot any small unconscious movements that act as leakage?
- Now write down your conclusions again about the people you've been watching. What is their mood? Relationship? Feelings?

- Then write down your analysis: Why did you think those things? What visual clues gave you those impressions?

These exercises will teach you how to give your 'perception muscles' an instant work-out. At this stage you shouldn't worry about being 'right' or 'wrong' in your assumptions or summaries. All you are doing here is beginning to understand how much or how little you notice when you look at other people.

It's very likely you'll find this exercise hard to do. This is because we all see different things when we look at people. Much of what you notice is linked to your own values or interests. One person might remember what a person was wearing, another might have seen skin colour and texture, or colour of hair or eyes. Someone on a diet might focus on the size of the hips. Your initial assessment could be biased towards wealth, style, personality or even sexual attraction, depending on your personal priorities.

You need to learn to view and assess *without prejudice*. This means hunting for clues about a person's thoughts and feelings without being misdirected by, for example, the cost of their jewellery or the colour of their tie. While these details can help give clues about the overall personality, they should be assessed equally with all the other visual signals on display.

CLUSTER SIGNALS

By watching characters on TV you will have begun to get used to making your assessments by reading their 'cluster signals', that raft of non-verbal messages that need to be balanced one against the other to make an overall decision.

This is vital for your success at the poker table. In real life we have time to make an appraisal regarding someone's personality or thoughts. We normally get the chance to make an instant evaluation, and then can change our opinion as we assimilate more clues. Much of the time it doesn't really matter whether we truly like or trust the person we're reading. They could be a stranger in the street or a work associate and often the situation isn't critical or instantaneous.

When you play poker, though, you have to make some very quick calls that could be worth a large pot of money. By honing your skills of perception and assimilation like this you'll soon learn how to make accurate quick-fire judgements based on early impressions and limited information.

ANALYSING GUT REACTIONS

For this stage of advanced reading we're going to go beyond the first impression.

Exercise 3

Take a look at the qualities and attributes you wrote down about your reality TV models. Now work through the footage slowly and carefully, this time working out *why* you came to those conclusions. What was it they *did* that made you think what you thought? This is a major step in making your subconscious conclusions conscious. Once you can do that you can be far more objective and much more accurate in your readings. For instance, at the first viewing you may have written on your notes that the subjects looked nervous. Now go back and review exactly what it was they did to make you think that.

- Did their breathing become shallow and more rapid?
- Did they start to sweat?
- Did their self-comfort or fiddling gestures increase?
- Did you notice subtle muscle tension or did their vocal tone rise a few notes?
- Maybe their blink rate increased or their eyes started to dart.

You are now looking for the symptoms on which to base your diagnosis. As you review your original evaluation, keep in mind your conscious assessment of the symptoms. You might want to change or modify your views. For instance, you might have thought that your subject looked tense. When you searched for the 'why' to that thought, you might now realise it was because sweat appeared on his forehead. But then you remember he was sitting under hot lights. By consciously considering these facts you might decide to delete that symptom from your list.

PERFORMED OR REAL?

During this stage of training you're going to learn to differentiate between genuine body language signals and performance gestures.

Exercise 4

People present themselves in different ways: their ideal 'selected image' is how they choose to sell themselves to the rest of the world. Their 'selected image' is usually signalled by:

- Clothing.

- Make-up.
- Hair style (and colour, if dyed).
- Perfume or aftershave.
- Tattoos.
- Car.
- Bag.
- Jewellery.

Then there are the 'learned traits' that may have been accentuated but which are less conscious and so far less likely to be adopted at will, such as:

- Eye contact.
- Type of smile.
- Handshake.
- Eye movement.
- Gestures.
- Posture.
- Walk.
- Accent.
- Tone of voice.

Finally there are the 'non-selected traits' that we have little if any control over but which create a visual impression of us nevertheless, such as:

- Sex.
- Age.
- Size.
- Colour.
- Features.

- Nervous tics.
- Leakage gestures.

The best footage to use for this is the first arrival of the *Big Brother* housemates into the house, a tough session of Prime Minister's Question Time, or a minister getting grilled in the studio. These subjects will all be displaying two types of body language signals: 'real' and 'performed'. By studying the TV footage at your leisure, you'll see the differences between the two and this will be invaluable training for spotting the bluff in poker.

Start slowly and work at your own analytical pace, then speed up the process until you can read much of the information from little more than a glance. Or work it out via your peripheral vision alone.

Spotting performance gestures

First you need to look for 'performance gestures'. These signal the subject's 'ideal' image message. Politicians being grilled are easy. You can assume they'll want to look calm and in control. So how will their 'performance gestures' reveal this? One big give-away will be that these signals will be especially strong at the moment the politician 'goes public' – that is, when they start to speak or first realise that the cameras are turned on them. The results can be especially telling.

When President Clinton faced a tribunal over the Monica Lewinsky affair, he sat looking vaguely angry and anxious until the moment he was told the questioning was about to begin. Perhaps not realising the cameras had been running all the time, he then adopted an 'innocent' facial expression, putting much more effort into raising his brows and widening his eyes than he had while sitting stormy-faced a few seconds before.

Gordon Brown often sports a dour expression, right up to the point when he is introduced verbally, and then he will adopt the 'lightning smile'. This full-voltage but very sudden grin looks totally at odds with the grim look of a few moments before, and requires far more effort.

Oscar nominees whose faces remain on screen while the winner is announced show almost industrial strength to force a smile and a laugh when another's name has been announced as winner. With all of these expressions, it's easy to spot the 'performance gestures' because they're the ones requiring all the effort.

Spotting 'leakage' gestures

The second stage is to search for the smaller 'leakage' gestures. These are the ones that happen more spontaneously and involve parts of the body that are the most difficult to control, such as the feet, fingers and eyes.

If we wear our emotions on our sleeve then it's the smaller gestures that tend to be the biggest give-aways. If these smaller and more fleeting movements tell the same story as the 'performed' gestures then it's likely that the subject is being honest with you at that moment. This is 'congruent communication', especially if the words, tone of voice and non-verbal communicators all send out the same message.

Often, though, we are 'incongruent' in our communication and when you learn to study other people you need to examine their incongruent tendencies in a conscious way. The bigger the discrepancy between the different signals the more you can assume your opponents are bluffing.

Joining the dots

Once you've got the hang of comparing the bigger 'performance' gestures with the smaller 'leakage' movements you can start to speed up the process. Look at posture, facial expression, spread of the limbs and the smile or lack of it. Then see if the smile extends to the eyes, if the fingers are fiddling or feet tapping. Do they lick their lips or are they swallowing more than normal? Is their breathing shallow and frequent or has their blink-rate increased? And just how big is the difference between the emotions behind the performance and the leakage?

After a while, once you have started to scan in a focused way you'll find you can summarise more easily and more quickly. There is no guarantee that your eventual conclusions will be accurate but they'll have a better hit rate than working on instinct alone.

Exercise 5

For this exercise, again study the week's TV viewing to pick out any interviews that you think might look interesting. Don't worry about the subject-matter: it could be sports or politics or even celebrity gossip. Record the interviews, but this time study them in three stages.

1. First, cast a speedy eye over the performance and try to decide via gut reaction whether the interviewee is being truthful or not. (Or maybe they're being good in parts, like the curate's egg.)
2. On second viewing, look for proof to back up your assumptions. View in slow motion, if necessary, and discover exactly what you have picked up to make you come to that conclusion about, say, the person's honesty.

3. On third viewing, go back and look without prejudice and re-assess your opinions. Now that you've studied the evidence in detail would you change your mind about this person's honesty? Is it possible that the expression or gesture that created your first impression has a more innocuous cause?

TV poker

Of course you can also watch real poker games on the television. Once you've mastered the knack of observing ordinary people, watching it will be useful to progress to studying the real thing.

REAL-LIFE 'STARING'

Modern life can be hectic and time is short and this often means you miss out on a lot of opportunities for 'people-watching'. Why walk down the corridor to talk to a colleague when you can send an e-mail instead? Why tell your partner face-to-face that you love her when a text is quicker? Why visit friends when you can phone?

Of all forms of communication, talking face-to-face is often the last option on the list. Why? Speed is one reason but shyness or embarrassment are common factors as well. We avoid talking directly to people when our message is difficult. This is often why work colleagues use e-mail as the ideal tool for sending communications they would find too challenging to deliver in person. E-mail and text messages have created a climate of anonymous communication that has awakened the assertive/aggressive/bold/romantic/flirtatious giant within.

But this has been achieved to the detriment of our visual communication skills. When we stop viewing we miss out on at least 50 per cent of the real meaning of the communicated message. There is no subtlety in an e-mail or text. The reader is left to imagine the true emotional meaning and therefore falls prey to interpretation risks.

To hone the skill of reading people you have to get out there and mix with them and communicate with them face-to-face. The more time you spend reading people in the flesh the easier it gets.

Be objective

Humans often suffer from what's called 'cognitive dissonance' – ignoring the evidence of our eyes because we don't like the message they're sending us. Often we prefer to believe the lie. When you play poker the lie will be a given, so thinking otherwise will create a loser mentality.

Look for patterns

Once you've upped your perception techniques you can start learning how to look for small behaviour patterns. These are going to be useful to you when you play poker as one of the best ways to read someone's thoughts and feelings is to spot small changes in these behaviour patterns.

When Michael Howard fought the 2005 general election as leader of the Conservative party he made a lot of speeches. I watched and analysed many of them. After monitoring a couple of these speeches it was easy to spot his 'signature gestures'. These are the movements he used for emphasis when addressing an audience.

One of his most frequently used gestures was a combination that I called 'beach ball and precision'. When he spoke about a problem the country was facing his hands would appear to mould an invisible beach ball in front of him. Then he would come up with his party's solution and use a finger-pinch gesture to show how the Tories were the only ones who had all the answers.

Once the election was over, he made one more speech to his party. Everyone expected him just to thank them for all their hard work and then get back to leading the opposition. As he spoke, though, I noticed one important difference. The 'beach ball' gesture was still there although the 'size' of the ball appeared to have grown. But the dramatic change was that there was no 'precision gesture' to back it up.

Michael Howard had run out of answers. I knew then that this was his resignation speech. A few moments later, one of his hands made a fluttery movement towards his face, which confirmed this for me. These small but dramatic changes in his body language patterns signalled very huge changes in his emotions and intentions.

Deviations are important. But to spot deviations you first have to become aware of the 'normal' patterns. To read someone closely you'll also have to look for 'atypical traits' or behaviours. While Michael Howard's beach-ball-minus-precision-gesture was a deviation from his normal behaviour, the fluttering hand was an atypical trait.

When Tony Blair started to sweat during a press conference in 2006, it was relatively atypical and caused column inches to be written speculating whether he was stressed or intending to stand down in favour of Gordon Brown. Although he famously soaked a shirt during a speech some years before, his normally calm, confident demeanour was seen to be the norm and therefore this deviation led to speculation.

Gordon Brown's body language patterns are equally set. When making a speech he will normally straighten and re-straighten his notes throughout the first third to half of his speech. If any other speaker started this ritual you would assume he or she was nervous to the point of terrified. With Gordon Brown it is the normal pattern, though, and some of his most powerful speeches have started with this obsessive, stressed-looking gesture. If he stopped doing it you'd be right to think something was up.

Like a big court case, there is a barrel-load of evidence to take into consideration and balance with the facts before we should come to any conclusions about our own view of someone's honesty.

Detection apprehension

When you're monitoring a subject's body language responses and they're aware you're doing so, you'll very likely prompt them to change their behaviour and so deviate from their normal patterns.

You probably change your own body language patterns if you are self-conscious, for example when going through customs at an airport. There's nothing worse than trying to feign normality when you know the officials are looking for signs of guilty behaviour. You probably have nothing in your luggage that should be declared but it doesn't matter. By this stage your 'detection apprehension' system has kicked in, regardless of guilt or innocence, and your new body language resembles that of a Great Train Robber returning from an awayday on the Costa del Sol.

However, when you're playing poker you can use 'detection apprehension' in your favour. If opponents believe you to be skilled in the art of reading them and spotting bluffs their 'detection apprehension' may increase. If other players are normally adept bluffers they may make body language errors that give you the clues you need.

Be careful how and when you use this technique, though. Sometimes there will be more to gain if your opponent is not on full alert. I'd suggest you do a lot of surreptitious player-watching first, to learn all you can about normal body language behaviour patterns. Then trigger the 'detection apprehension' response later, at a crucial point in the game. (You could let slip that you've read this book.)

To stare or not to stare?

That *is* the question. There is a perceived wisdom among professional poker players that staring an opponent out is a very useful technique. The starer looks powerful and intimidates the opponent. It creates what they think is a 'Derren Brown moment', making victims feel their mind is being read and placing them under so much pressure that they're unable to perform effectively.

For a heavyweight boxer, this type of toe-to-toe staring can be useful. It implies physical intimidation and can undermine an opponent's confidence to the point where he or she is unable to fight to the best of their ability.

For a poker player, though, the technique needs to be re-examined – for three reasons:

1. Staring is not the same as watching. Trying to stare in a very obvious and intimidating manner means you're not being as perceptive as you would be if you monitored your opponent in a more relaxed manner, with a glance.
2. Intimidation might not be your most useful objective. To play poker well you need to be able to spot the bluff. To do

that you need to study subtle changes in your opponents' body language. If opponents are being stared at they are likely to change their behaviour in a very erratic way. They might feel under pressure but exactly how that pressure might manifest itself is anybody's guess. They might take more risks or become more cautious.

3. Your opponent could see your stare as a challenge and stare back at you. This will lead to a stand-off that is all about power-posturing and nothing about winning the pot. It is at this point most sane people would think any joy in the game has evaporated. Staring is dominant behaviour but only if you're going into some type of physical battle. Otherwise it's just chest-beating nonsense.

If I played poker for money I'd probably let everyone know that I was a professional body language mind-reader. This would unsettle them and shake out a few clumsy attempts at cover-ups. However, I'd only try this for a one-hit game. If I were playing more frequently I'd throw this ace card down more strategically.

The ideal technique is to watch your opponents for much of the play without making them feel they're being monitored. This is easy. Staring involves what is called 'dead-eye'. The eyes watch the other person, following their every move but remaining expressionless, which is what makes a stare intimidating. The blank stare appears to have no other purpose. This induces paranoia in the victim. The starer is showing no signs of approval or friendship, therefore he or she must be watching critically. By staring he or she is trying to signal those critical opinions in a threatening way.

The answer is to soften your eye expression. There's no need to produce a smile but by relaxing the tiny muscles around your eye as you allow your gaze to rest on your opponents you appear pleasantly interested rather than critical and threatening. Imagine you like them and allow that emotion to reflect in your eye expression. Think 'polite' rather than 'rival'.

Be aware of your blink rate. This needs to look as normal as possible. Remember that the tension of brewing conflict or competition will accelerate your blink rate. Staring and fast blinking is going to look like an act of open warfare. Gazing with a normal blink rate is going to look innocent. If you slow your blink rate down too much, though, you could end up looking like an owl.

Eye dart

Avoid darting eyes, too, which also gives the game away that you are studying the other players. For example, when players pick up their cards or touch their chips and your eyes flick round too quickly, your cover will be blown. You might just as well sit there with a copy of this book out on the table. There will be key moments in the game when you will want to study each player's movement, like when the cards are dealt or the chips stacked, but you must hone the art of looking without alerting.

9

HOW TO SPOT YOUR OPPONENTS' BODY LANGUAGE CLUES

Now you've learned all about perception and people-watching you can move on to the technique of translating what you see. This means people-reading without prejudice. The minute you allow prejudicial assumptions to affect your judgement your skills of perception will get in the way of a poker win.

When you look at someone for the first time, one of the first pieces of information you'll be searching for is whether or not that person is any threat to you. This is your 'survival response'. Much of this information is gleaned within the first couple of seconds. This process is called 'social encoding'.

SOCIAL ENCODING

Processing visual information about another person is a five-stage process:

1. *Scanning*: This is general looking without conscious analysis.
2. *Focusing*: This involves consciously identifying and analysing stimuli.
3. *Comprehension*: Now the brain puts meaning to what you see.
4. *Assimilation*: The information is linked to memories and knowledge.
5. *Response*: Finally you form a reaction to all of this.

This encoding occurs all the time but the only stages of the process you're probably aware of are the first and the last. You glance, you give your response. Someone walks into your office and you decide who they are, what they're like and why they're there without recognising stages two, three and four.

To improve your poker game you need to fill in the gaps and turn what is a subconscious process into a conscious one. Stop thinking about gut reactions, assumptions and 'feelings' or vibes and start being analytical. Once you become conscious of each stage and aware of your thinking or 'cognitive' processes you'll achieve a much higher degree of success. This more analytical view is called 'cognitive algebra'.

ASK YOURSELF 'WHY?'

The key word to use when you're trying to decipher your opponents' body language is: 'Why?' A gesture or movement is the only non-negotiable piece of information in the process. If they scratch the side of their head then they scratched the side of their head. Fact. Everyone who saw the gesture would agree to it and a judge would take it as incontrovertible evidence.

From there, though, the process of analysis begins to be random and subjective. Your brain assimilates several signals at once before it begins to jump to conclusions:

- Was the head tilted?
- Were they frowning as they scratched?
- Exactly what part of the head were they scratching?
- How rapid was the scratching?

The brain then tries to create historical links:

- When have I seen this gesture performed before?
- What did the gesture mean on that occasion?

The brain loves patterns because patterns make life easier and this in turn can lead to stereotyping and even prejudice, as in: 'When I've seen someone do that in the past it normally meant they were bored.' This is your brain interpreting a signal based on previous experience. But that experience could be flawed. Every gesture can have several different meanings. Perhaps they were bored or perhaps they just had an itchy scalp.

Now, whatever your interpretation, the next stage is crucial. This is where you make a judgement based on what you have seen and your interpretation of it. If you translated that scratching as boredom and *you* were the one speaking at the time, you would respond negatively, perhaps being annoyed at the scratcher. If someone else is speaking and you're bored you might feel empathy with the scratcher.

Turning chaos into structure

In poker you can't afford to use stereotypical thinking when reading your opponents. Many of your assumptions about their gestures might be based on flawed thinking. In reality TV, people are together for long periods of time and flawed assumptions often result in unnecessary conflict. A common problem is looking or staring. When housemates fall out it is often because they didn't like the way the others were looking at them.

But looking and eye movement can be cultural. Some people use more eye contact than others. Some cultures find eye contact challenging or insulting, a lack of respect. Others think it's rude if you don't look. The starer might think they're signalling friendliness or even attraction but the 'receiver' could find it intimidating.

When you study your opponents' body language you must avoid getting drawn into flawed patterns of thinking. So it's very important, not to say vital, that when you ask yourself, 'Why?' as in 'Why did they do that?' you keep an open mind. Then decide without prejudice. That way you avoid linking it to, for instance, something a schoolteacher used to do when you were nine years old, or an ex-partner's irritating habit that used to drive you crazy.

When I'm analysing someone's body language signals I use a three-way process:

1. First, I use gut reaction, just like everyone else. This feels like the psychic part of the process. Sometimes you just don't know how you know – but you do.
2. Second, I use logical analysis based on my own and others' research. What do these gestures mean when or if animals

use them? What is this gesture's pedigree? What is the scientific explanation for this movement?

3. Third, I try it out for myself. By copying a gesture or movement you can get inside the user's mind and understand their feelings, creating what can often be quite an intense feeling of empathy.

To be objective in your analysis, I suggest you tap into all of these, not just one. When you want to work out what a poker gesture means, they provide you with three clear voices. It might sound like a slow process but it doesn't have to be. Sometimes the three voices agree with one another and sometimes they don't. But at least you're making the decision based on all the information you can get, rather than allowing some dusty old assumptions that you've never bothered to question lead your thinking.

Knowing when to quit

It's good to have a fall-back position for those moments when you just can't puzzle out what's going on. There are always times and players that twist your mind into knots. Are they bluffing or double-bluffing or have they opted for the triple or quadruple bluff just to fool you?

When your opponent gets beyond clever and their body language is too confusing it's best just to let it drop. Go back to bald decisions based purely on the hand you're holding and the statistical chance it gives you of winning.

Forget the gurning or poker face across the table. Use what is about to happen as powerful knowledge, even if you don't employ it in your decision-making process this time around. Every movement or lack of it from your opponent will tell you something, especially once you know the outcome. You might have lost this hand but you can still analyse and store the memory of their behaviour for future use.

Imagine you're a goalie facing a penalty kick. Your opponent feigns to the left, you dive in that direction and the ball is slotted into the right side of the goal. Instead of beating yourself up for losing, better to store this away as one more fact you've learnt about your opponent. Their trick might have beaten you this time but they've also shown their hand, which makes it much more likely you'll get to the ball the next time they take a shot at a goal.

SPATIAL BEHAVIOUR

Another factor that you must take into account when analysing body language is the distance between you and the other players, your 'spatial zone'. This will have a bearing on your ability to read your opponents as it will affect:

- Your line of vision.
- Your own comfort and feelings about reading that other person.
- Their feelings about being watched, which can affect their body language signals, giving a false reading.

Space relates to power, comfort and safety. Most of the time we're unaware of the effects of spatial zones and distances but as soon as they get breached the immediate discomfort will often pull it from subconscious into conscious response.

HOW TO SPOT YOUR OPPONENTS' BODY LANGUAGE CLUES

Our whole lives are governed by spatial choreography. To adapt to modern life we have had to change the way we cope with crowded areas but that coping has led to a key evolution in our body language rituals. Instead of monitoring someone who is inappropriately close in order to check for safety and threat of attack, we now tend to avert our gaze.

When you get into a crowded lift or train, for instance, you will instinctively look away from your fellow passengers. This one simple signal is done to create social order in what any other animal would see as an untenable situation. In many ways it prevents us from attacking and being attacked by our fellow passengers. But this response won't work in your favour when you're playing poker. Where you sit at the table can be as important as how you play.

The first thing you need to keep in mind is that we have four key 'spatial zones'. The appropriateness of these zones depends on our relationship with the other person. They are:

1. *Intimate zone*: As the name suggests, this is the closest, ranging from touching distance to about 50 cm (18 in) away from the other person. This is reserved for very close friends, family or lovers (or very crowded public transport!). When you see two people communicating together in this zone in public it is usually regarded as appropriate to avert your gaze.
2. *Personal zone*: This ranges from about 50 cm (18 in) to 1.2 m (4 ft) away. By excluding people from this distance you seal yourself in a bubble of safety and comfort. At this distance, you feel protected and untouched by others.
3. *Social zone*: When other people are 1.2–3.6 m (4–12 ft) away, communication is more formal, for example at a business meeting or social gathering.

4. *Public zone*: This ranges from 3.6–7.5 m (12–25 ft). Needless to say, this is the 'safest' zone because we are close enough to monitor the other person but far enough to take action if we feel threatened in any way.

Status and space

We tend to stand closer to people we feel are our 'equals' in terms of status. We also tend to avoid moving closer to someone we feel is of higher status. The higher-status person, however, will feel free to move closer to us if they so choose.

Territory and invasion

When people gather there is always the matter of space-ownership. As soon as you take your seat you will start to mark your territory, often invisibly but sometimes physically by stacking your chips, or arranging your arms, hands or personal belongings around you on the table. On a subconscious level, everyone knows and understands the rules: the only piece of space you have a right to is your own. And in poker each space is equal. This is called 'spatial ownership'. If someone invades your space in any way they will be signalling their superiority.

This space invasion can be natural, accidental or deliberate. It can even look friendly, like someone placing an arm around the back of your chair. By studying the way another player sets out his or her space, you'll get a pretty good idea of how they might play and what sort of decisions they'll make.

So social encoding is a very special skill that involves focus and practice. The good news though is that you've already been doing it for most of your life. Unlike learning to drive a car or set the DVD to record a programme, you'll only be dusting down a talent you were born with and learning how to hone it and then put it into practice around the poker table.

10

TRUE OR FALSE?

It is vital to learn the skills of reading a bluff. Bluffing is what real poker is all about. Before you start to de-layer your way through all the bluff and double-bluff, though, the first thing you'll need to decipher is this: Are they bluffing at all? John Duthie:

'There are certain specific situations that arise in poker when it is likely that your opponent may be bluffing and the first thing to do is recognise that. Then you have to go through a very specific feeling process to get inside your opponent's head and just make a decision. You have to be wary of false tells. Players will often look away from you when they have a very strong hand, but if they know you know this then they will use it against you next time they play. I believe it all becomes instinctive and when you are playing well, you get it right and when you are playing badly you get it wrong.'

Bluffer types
Poker players can be divided into three groups. There are those who are prepared to bluff, who we'll call 'Performers', and those who are not, who we'll call 'Naturists'. Then there is a

third category. This is for players who take their performance to a higher level. They aim to bluff, double-bluff and even treble-bluff to confuse their opponents. We will call them 'High Performers'. These players are the ultimate risk-takers and they play for the adrenaline buzz as much as the pot. They enjoy a poor hand that they can bluff over even more than a good hand. These players use poker as an extreme sport. Often High Performers strive to look like Naturists and sometimes they really are acting naturally. High Performers play like chameleons.

Remember, there are two types of poker lies:

1. *Concealing the truth*: Masking natural emotions such as disappointment, frustration or glee in a poker face, or
2. *Performance lies*: Suppressing your natural emotions and acting out an emotion that you're not really feeling and which might be in direct contrast, such as looking smug over a weak hand or looking pleased when someone else wins.

Naturist or Performer?

Naturists are as rare as hens' teeth in the game of poker yet they do exist and you should be aware of them. They play the game as it comes. Why would anyone not bluff? Work it out for yourself. Perhaps they're just learning the game. Maybe they play strictly for fun. But even people who play for fun or are still learning to play will have a moment of epiphany when they realise it would be good to bluff.

Naturists rarely look what they are. The worst mistake you can make is to assume someone's a Naturist without checking for confirmation. The worst deceivers can be members of your own family who can suddenly and unexpectedly flex their 'bluff' muscles, often in an act of passive-aggressive behaviour. But if an apparent Naturist can bluff, and a bluffer can pretend to be a Naturist, then how can you tell which is which? There are several ways to see who is bluffing and who is being themselves.

Obviously, you're not going to ask another player if he or she is being honest. And even if you did they wouldn't dream of giving an honest answer. So, your 'questions' must be non-verbal. These are like sonic mating calls that will receive a response from the other player. By their degree of response you will be able to predict whether they are acting or not during the game.

The technique you'll be using is one we've briefly mentioned, called 'mirroring'. It's largely a subconscious process – when two people feel a bond or empathy they adopt postures and movements that mirror each other. It's rife during cultural events and poker is a key cultural event. Only this time you'll be 'leading' – that is, instigating movements to see if he or she follows suit. In the normal world, mirroring should be natural. If you know the other players well you should expect a high level of mirroring, if they are behaving normally. If you're playing with strangers you should still get some sort of response, such as a smile.

When you throw out a small and genuine-looking smile to someone it's very hard for them not to 'catch' it. It's important that your smile isn't stretched or false-looking. If you perform this type of smile around the poker table the odds are it will be seen as sarcastic or aggressive and the other players will just look away quickly to prove they are not going to be intimidated.

But a sweet, supportive smile is another thing. Ping that one out and the only person who doesn't return it is going to be the one who's set on 'permanent performance' mode. You could do the same thing with a small raise of the eyebrows. This friendly-looking 'tie-sign' (a subtle, non-verbal signal that links you with the recipient) is innocuous enough and should be returned by anyone who is behaving with some degree of normality. If it gets blanked you receive an immediate clue that this player is not behaving normally and is therefore going to be acting while playing.

The Trojan Horse

What if you suspect players are bluffing or double-bluffing? Should you let them know you're onto them? Possibly not. If you act suspicious they'll be on the alert. If you act as though you've been suckered in they'll relax and continue – and maybe become careless. This is what police interrogators call 'The Trojan Horse', allowing liars to believe their lie is working in an effort to get to the truth. You can do this throughout a game or as long as you play with the bluffer. When you put people under pressure it gets difficult to tell between the signals caused by the pressure of examination and the signals caused by the pressure of telling a lie.

Researchers at Portsmouth University claim that liars have to think harder. When we think hard we often need to keep still to concentrate. However, expansive gestures are not only common but likely, possibly in an attempt to disguise our stillness, such as when Clinton jabbed a finger when saying he 'did not have sexual relations with that woman'.

And speaking of women . . . females often make better High

Performers because they tend to wave their hands around as they talk more than men, which distracts from or masks the lie. When men exaggerate their hand movements, for added emphasis, it tends to look incongruent (false), which is why many male politicians struggle to look convincing as they employ all those emphatic gestures when making a speech.

Poker player Simon Freedman admits women can be tricky players: *'I do prefer playing with all men. In many ways it's all about how clever and powerful you are. I haven't worked women out in 40 years, let alone at the poker table. Blokes are easier to work out.'*

GIVE-AWAYS

I'm now going to briefly review the most common signals that are seen as 'give-aways' to remind you what to look for. Remember, never look at an opponent's body language just to confirm that your own assumptions are right. Look with an open mind. Look without prejudice. Consider every possibility before you act.

- *Face-touching*: When you lie you tend to want to touch your face. This is a subconscious attempt to mask your lies. But face-touching can be prompted by many other factors like boredom, shyness and anxiety.
- *False smile*: Most smiles are fake. You use them as a form of social grooming. But if your opponent smiles you could get clues about its provenance if you look at its shape. A natural smile is relatively speedy and symmetrical. However, a 'lightning smile' that flicks on and off will be

fake. Fake smiles can also be slower and more lop-sided. The muscles around the eye create laughter lines if the smile is genuine.

- *No eye expression*: Most people have many expressions visible in their eyes so if the eye looks devoid of expression you could assume this deadpan look means they're into 'shut-down mode' and doing a poker face. But keep in mind it could be their normal expression. Some people have naturally dead-fish eyes so you need to make comparisons. Also discover whether your opponent has had Botox anti-wrinkle injections recently. Botox freezes the muscles, leading to what can be an unnatural 'zombie' look.

- *Eye movement*: If your opponents look away at the moment of what could be a lie or bluff you could assume you're being deceived. The eyes are a 'Grade A' give-away. By putting down the shutters, even for a second, your opponents may think they can hide the lie. But you need to take the effect of your staring into account. When you're under scrutiny you'll often look guilty even when you're as innocent as the day is long. Most people think liars avert their eyes when they lie. In fact, liars are more likely to increase eye contact – to 'brazen out' the lie.

- *Pupil dilation and rapid eye movement*: Your opponents' pupils will widen when pleased with their hand and narrow when displeased. If their eyes dart about it could mean indecision or borderline panic. However, an inexperienced player could display panic for reasons other than a poor hand.

- *Direction of gaze*: This can signal intention – where we look is where we really want to be. For example, looking at the door might signal a desire to make an escape. But perhaps they're expecting a friend or another player? Maybe they're claustrophobic.

- *Hesitation*: If opponents pause too long before speaking or betting they could well be preparing a lie or bluff. However, this also needs to be seen in context. Are they tired or distracted? Are they new to the game and nervous?

- *Foot tapping*: This metronomic gesture shows your opponent's preferred pace or rhythm. You could read this as impatience to end the lie and get away. But could there be other reasons for that impatience? When do they tap their foot? If they're tapping while others are playing it could be eagerness to win.

- *Crossed arms or legs*: Folded arms can signal defensiveness and worry about what will happen if your opponent gets caught out. But do look at the timing. If they fold their arms after playing, it could signal relaxation. Arms that are folded high across the chest can mean aggression and challenge.

- *Facial twitch or tic*: This is unlikely to be voluntary. Some face muscles aren't under conscious control and a very quick tic or twitch may occur if they bluff or lie. If it's a performed twitch or tic that they're using to bluff it's likely to be clumsy to the point of looking hilarious. If it's well-crafted they almost deserve to win for the effort they must have put in rehearsing prior to the game.

- *Blushing*: The increased heart rate prompted by a bluff could cause the face to redden as blood rushes to capillaries in the skin. This is often triggered by 'lie anticipation' and might start well before it's their turn but soon after their cards are inspected or dealt. But it could be blushing caused by shyness or a hot flush.

- *Micro-expressions*: When your opponents lie or bluff they could display very fleeting expression changes or flickers of expression. These can be quite telling but you need to know how to interpret them. A forward tongue poke can be an expression of disgust but a lick of the lips or mouth might indicate they're savouring the moment.

- *Body language waffle*: Waving the arms or other exaggerated gestures that have no verbal point can be a symptom of lying. However, it could be cultural gesturing.

- *Redirecting attention*: Distracting gestures could imply your opponent is trying to hide the lie or hide any potential chinks in their bluff techniques. However, it could also mean nervousness prompted by inexperience, or plain boredom.

- *Fidgeting*: When an opponent starts to fidget it's likely you'll begin to think they're bluffing. However, even this classic lie signal can be misleading. Monitor when it occurs and what type of movement is involved before you come to any conclusion.

- *Conflicting signs*: Any contradiction between what your opponent says and what their body language signals imply is called 'incongruence'. It is one of the best ways to unmask a bluff in poker. But make sure you're interpreting those signals correctly. The bigger, more visible gestures are likely to be part of your opponent's performance. Smaller conflicting signals will usually be the truth. So if your opponent's posture looks confident and they are smiling but their feet are twitching under the table you should read the smaller signals and act accordingly. This combination would mean they're bluffing by pretending a weak hand is a strong one.

- *Sweating*: Excess sweat can be produced when the adrenaline pumps faster round the body. It suggests lie-prompted anxiety but – you've guessed it – it could just mean your opponent is hot.
- *Gulping and swallowing*: This increases during moments of tension but you'll need to decipher other signals to see whether this is prompted by nerves or excitement. The frequency of swallowing will change under the pressure of a lie.

Vocalising emotion

If you look for emotion in the voice you'll get a clue as to whether your opponent is bluffing or not. For example, a sudden rise in vocal tone, known as 'pitch switch', will mean the vocal cords have tightened, meaning stress. But this could be caused by win anticipation as well as negative stress. Look for confirmation. But what if the player speaks in a monotone, deliberately hiding all emotion or feeling?

Airline pilots speak in a monotone to give a sense of strength, calm and professionalism. Even if a plane is primed to crash-land you will often hear on the black box flight recorder that the pilots employed a low-pitch monotone to show they were in control and therefore acting calmly to divert an emergency. Army officers are taught to use a military monotone so that they sound calm under fire.

TV presenters, on the other hand, are trained to add 'energy' to their tones and overstate excitement and enthusiasm to beef up the programme content. I always thought I had a pitchy voice that erred on the side of childlike excitement until I did my first voice-over for my TV series on body language. After wittering on for a few moments I was asked to give it more energy and this was the only coaching I had. In the end I stood up and waved my arms in my usual style to inject the appropriate amount of enthusiasm into my voice.

The clue you will need if you're dealing with a monotone player is whether he or she normally talks like this. If not then you can assume they've adopted the 'poker voice' effect in an attempt to bluff or lie. But it could just be nerves.

And what if the tone and pitch do change, becoming higher or more strained? This is usually the result of tension or stress. Great! Then that means they're bluffing? No, it just means they're tense or stressed. What you now need to ascertain is whether that stress is prompted by 'lie anxiety', 'discovery anxiety' or a need to go to the loo.

Symbolic gestures

There are several body language gestures that are as precise as words. These are gestures we use in place of words. They may be insulting or offensive, like the V-sign or the middle-finger jab, or dismissive, like the head-shake or the shrug. When these gestures are intentional they're used like sign-language. When they're unintentional, though, they are a form of leakage and can give fascinating insights into the 'speaker's' state of mind. So how can you tell the intentional from the leakage?

Often leaked gestures are performed in a semi-hidden way. For instance the 'speaker' might hold his or her fingers in a V-sign but rest their hand on their thigh or the side of their face rather than holding the gesture aloft. Or it could be half-baked, raising an eyebrow rather than shrugging a shoulder. When you spot the symbolic gesture emerging as leakage you can usually trust it as being indicative of the player's true feelings, so if the V-sign occurs when you place your bet you can assume the other player is registering irritation at you and that you've beaten them.

TRUE OR FALSE?

Illustrative gestures

When we talk normally and truthfully we will often use illustrative hand gestures to describe our words. Some people (like me) do this frequently and extensively while others do it occasionally, when they feel strongly about something or are trying to explain or describe something. Illustrative gestures are mime gestures. If you told someone you had a small child you might use a hand to indicate his height from the ground. If you were telling someone you need an A4 sheet of paper your hands would be out in front of you, like an angler describing a catch.

You're trying to describe what you see in your mind using your hands. Therefore gestures are usually true. If you play against someone who normally employs the illustrative gesture and they decrease at some point you can assume they're bluffing.

Self-comfort gestures

These are gestures that indicate inner turmoil, such as self-grooming, fiddling with cuffs or tie, scratching, smoothing clothes, hair-twirling or stroking, tooth-picking, nail-biting, pen-twirling, tooth-cleaning gestures. They're often seen as a sign of lying – but be careful. There are several situations that might prompt these symptoms. By opting for self-comfort gestures opponents are letting you know they're anxious. But that anxiety could be mild or acute. It could be prompted by a weak hand or the fact that they've left the TV on at home. Like all other body language signals or gestures, you'll have to put them into context. When did they start? Do they increase at certain times? Are there patterns to those times?

However, when someone is bluffing these self-comfort gestures will be the first to go, as a conscious decision. They're top of the list of what people believe to be a liar's repertoire and an experienced liar will always look to suppress them.

So, remember to look beyond the obvious or clichéd signs of lie or bluff behaviour.

11

PERSONALITY AND BEHAVIOUR TYPES

When you play poker regularly you'll see many different behaviour types. Sometimes these classifications will be obvious from your opponents' behaviour outside the game. So if you know your opponents well it would be easy to assume you'll know their style of play already. But the side of the personality that is exposed during a game of poker might be suppressed at other times. It could even be a surprise to your opponents! Use this chapter to judge their playing style and therefore be better placed to predict the moves and decisions they'll make.

It can be dangerous to stereotype other people and yet this behaviour grid has been produced to help understand and even predict a character's behaviour in general but especially in regard to how they will play poker.

Behavioural patterns are created in childhood and may remain with us throughout our lives. Often they are impossible to change or conceal, even when there is no obvious reward in using them.

One of the core behavioural patterns will be associated with winning or losing. It's not hard to see how this relates to childhood. Small children are very focused negotiators and game-players. For them the idea of getting what they want out of a situation is of prime importance. For a child, nothing else matters, even if all they want is sweets or a sticker – something an adult would find no big deal.

For some people, this focus on the win tends to desert them as they grow up, mainly because they develop empathy and realise that winning creates losers and so start to imagine how losing must feel. However, competitive people carry the intense urge to win through to adulthood. Sports people, for example, are taught to fixate on the win and give it their total, obsessive focus.

Playing poker is very much the same deal. You're all there to win and the win is very obvious. In poker there are no second prizes or also-rans. Nobody gets a medal for coming third. The win is almost as intense as it is for children wanting chocolate. So under these hothouse conditions it is very easy to see the ghosts of childhood emerging from beneath layers of social training and masking. Sometimes these behaviours will surprise the people suffering from them. But they should never be a surprise to the opponent. Use this behaviour grid to gain insights into your opponent's play 'type'. As you can see, there are four main behaviour types: 'Drivers', 'Expressives', 'Empathists' and 'Analysts', and they'll often behave in predictable ways when they are winning, losing and bluffing.

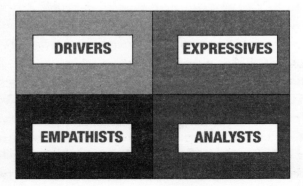

DRIVERS

These are natural poker-players and will often dominate a game. They are primarily task-focused and impatient so the speed of the game will appeal to them and you may see signs of impatience if other players take their time deciding on a move. Drivers use high-impact but concise communication patterns. They'll talk loudly and clearly but shy away from chatter or small-talk. Fiercely competitive, they'll need to celebrate a win in what might be an openly gloating way, punching the air or shouting, maybe even doing a small dance of victory.

When Drivers are winning

Of all the four behaviour types, winning is of highest importance to Drivers. It's their core motivational reward and they may do anything to ensure success. These are ruthless, focused winners but that doesn't mean their game is particularly clever or accurate. Power and status are vital and will be the two things they struggle to mask after a win. Their main emotional focus will be based around the win and this makes them quite vulnerable to a good body language reader.

Having to be the best at everything also means being the best bluffer and dominant player. Often what they see as cleverness and cunning is in fact their greatest weakness. They will often try to psych out other players by boasting about their techniques. This is a bad move as it alerts people to their bluffs. This is the group most likely to boast about their body language skills. Expect:

- Jumping up.
- Shouting 'Yes! Yes! Yes!'

- Punching the air.
- Football-style goal-scoring celebratory routines and rituals.
- Immediate claiming of chips or money.
- Laughter as the pot is pulled close.
- A need to get the pot close to the torso.
- Kissing the chips.
- Smile of contempt.

When Drivers are losing

This is when the pressure really mounts. Just as Drivers find it hard to mask their delight and superiority signals when they win, so they'll struggle to hide their disappointment at losing. Drivers are very bad losers. If they're unmasked they will display very open signs of frustration or anger such as throwing down cards or chips, looking away as the winner takes the pot, pushing their chair away from the table and even walking away from the game.

If they look at the other players their gaze is likely to be accusatory. Drivers find it very hard to accept responsibility for losing and will seek to blame others. This means their eyes will dart from one player to another after they lose, trying to manufacture an excuse that will lift the blame from their own shoulders.

They will often adopt a critical tone, using words like 'You should have . . .' 'Your mistake was . . .' 'Why did you . . .?' and any other version of that bad-losing child. There is a very strong Alpha male/female identity for Drivers and the Alpha loser is a very bad masker. Expect:

- Darting, accusing eyes.
- Jaw tension, clenched teeth.
- Removing themselves from the table.

- A strong out-take of breath.
- Sulk signals, jutting lower lip, drop in vocal tone.
- Shouting.
- Fear smile.
- Thumping table in mimic of win behaviour.

When Drivers are bluffing

Of all the types, Drivers will have the least problem with bluffing as their guilt levels are very low. However, their need to be seen as dominant and powerful means that they struggle when they have to play down delight at winning or frustration at losing. When Drivers are bluffing they'll usually work in the style of the Mississippi riverboat gambler, producing a performance that is part poker face and part intimidation. There will be no pretence of lack of experience or knowledge in a bid to fool their opponents. Drivers are far more likely to pretend to be better and more experienced players than their opponents.

Drivers are capable of placing very large bets and these will get even larger when they bluff. A common ploy for Drivers is to study their cards then look slowly at each of their opponents, employing steady eye contact, and a hint of a smirk. They love the turn-on of confusing other people as this gives them a feeling of power. They need to see that confusion, though, so will rarely avert their eyes. Expect:

- Deepening of the voice.
- Spreading out in the chair.
- Body staying static.
- Body sitting straight on the chair.
- Increased use of eye contact – even staring.
- Trace of a smirk.

- Eyes throwing out a direct challenge to opponent.
- Increase in confidence gestures.
- Change in breathing patterns – watch the chest as breathing becomes more shallow and frequent.
- A muscle working at the side of the face.

EXPRESSIVES

These are 'High Performers'. Expressives get bored easily and love the short-burst high-octane excitement of the game. Their strength lies in their ability to act and they love being the centre of attention as they perform, so are unlikely to bring any subtlety to their behaviour. Whereas Drivers and/or Analysts (see pages 171 and 179) can suppress their gestures and play 'poker face', this approach would be a struggle for Expressives. They prefer to misdirect via their performances, pretending to have a good hand when they have a poor one and vice versa. Expressives are starters but not finishers and their low attention-span and dislike of detail or analysis makes them very impulsive players who are happy to take risks.

When Expressives are winning

The win is only a reward for Expressives if it ensures they get more attention, so they like to discuss their own win and hear other players describe their win in a blow-by-blow account. Expressives are fond of patter and chatter although they're not good listeners and get distracted easily. Expect:

- Increase in patter.
- Increase in jokes and wisecracks.

- More laughter.
- Speech becoming more staccato.
- Shoulders starting to rise.
- Increase in body movement.
- Sucking in of lips.

When Expressives are losing

As we've seen, Expressives don't only play for the win but also for the fun of playing and the excuse for a get-together that provides them with an audience. However, they can be very sore losers, albeit for different reasons than Drivers. Expressives struggle with the idea that someone else is the centre of attention and may well respond like a naughty child craving attention. Expect:

- Poking fun at winner.
- Leaning over or standing close to winner.
- Touching winner.
- Making jokes about winner to other players.
- Slumping and going quiet.
- Look of misery (mouth down-turned at corners or chin-shrug).

When Expressives are bluffing

The life of Expressives is one huge bluff as they generally fail to prepare or be thorough about work, preferring to wing it. But they also make brilliant performers and sales people. For Expressives, bluffing is all part of the fun. This makes them able to relax into the role whereas Drivers will sit on a hotbed of suppressed aggression. The biggest struggle for Expressives will be performing a deadpan bluff. This goes against their entire persona and they'll only adopt it for one of two reasons:

1. To pull off a double-bluff.
2. To get a laugh. This means their poker face will soon start to crack, which will leave you with a dilemma. By allowing the mask to slip and so announcing their attempt at a bluff, are they going to revert to displays of truth? Is the exposé as obvious as it looks?

The clues will lie in the level of intelligence and cunning of the Expressives in question. They may slip roles several times during one hand. If they're borderline stupid you can believe what you see – they were attempting to bluff with a bad hand but couldn't keep the poker face in place. If they're clever they could be almost totally unpredictable. Remember, they won't have any game plan, they're just making it up as they go along. The performance is probably confusing them as much as other players. Look for signs of body language leakage to work out what's really going on. Study the lower half of the body if you can – this is their weakest part for role-play. Expect:

- Suppression gestures. Expressives are such natural performers that they might have to physically restrain themselves.
- Sitting on hands.
- Gripping table.
- Odd moments of small rocking movements.
- Diversion gestures – sipping water, looking away, humming, all to distract from the performance and give the Expressive's poker face a rest.

EMPATHISTS

Of all the groups, Empathists have the hardest struggle to become truly great poker players as they are motivated mostly by relationships and would be happier with a social game involving teams. Empathists like the company of others and so the idea of being 'poker faced' or ruthless in their play is a challenge for them. They're most likely to give themselves away with 'denial gestures', small expressions or movements that show the bluff. For Empathists, it's important to be liked and so if they bluff they have an overwhelming desire to send out subconscious signals to say they're only acting. Honesty is important to Empathists. They also hate to discover that another player has been bluffing. They play at a very personal level and so are both bad losers and bad winners. Their core strength is their ability to focus on other people and be a good watcher and listener. Although they make poor performers they're good at reading other people. Their high levels of interest and perception means they're good at picking out a bluff.

When Empathists are winning

Empathists are natural team-players and back-seat drivers and so are uncomfortable with a winning streak. They dislike the attention it brings and are happiest passing on the baton and even helping to coach someone else to be a better player. Expect:

- Signals of exasperation when opponents show bad hands, even jokingly accusing them of dropping out too soon or not laying their hand correctly.
- Offering advice to opponents.

- Making small movements towards opponents as though trying to see their hand and help them.
- Increased self-comfort or fiddling gestures.
- Pulling their winnings towards them with great reluctance and then ignoring them.
- Less eye contact.
- Use of dismissive gestures like waving hands or shaking head.

When Empathists are losing

It would be easy to think that Empathists are likely to jump onto the table to celebrate when they lose but that's not so. Despite their generosity and desire for relationships Empathists are very sensitive to criticism and may react in a negative way if they feel they have failed. Expect:

- Raising cards to use as a shield.
- Body barrier gestures, self-hug, arm across body, crossed legs.
- Biting lips.
- Nail chewing.
- Puffing.
- Nervous smiling.
- Increased blink rate.

When Empathists are bluffing

Empathists won't relish bluffing other players as it goes against their core values, especially honesty. However, their skills of perception and empathy means they're uncannily good players if they can overcome their sense of guilt. It's easy to underestimate

Empathists and categorise them as touchy-feely and submissive. This isn't always true. They can be very good at game-playing and very good at knowing exactly which tactics will work on who. The quickest way to spot an Empathist's bluff is to flash them a small but rather pathetic smile of misery. If he or she looks away quickly they're holding the winning hand. If they smile back in sympathy they've got a low hand. Expect:

- The unexpected. Empathists are capable of performing very clever bluffs.
- Subtle rather than over-egged bluffs.
- Subtle changes in behaviour (which won't seem so subtle once you've studied them).
- Signals of stress at making the performance.
- Shoulder tension, a change in breathing, frowning.
- Reduction in eye contact.
- Reluctance to read you if you make them feel guilty. If you're someone who boasts or enjoys beating others, Empathists will be comfortable watching your pain. But if you're the underdog they will find it hard to win against you.

ANALYSTS

Analysts value logic and detail above all other aspects of the game. They're slow and methodical and need to take their time without being rushed or pushed to make a decision. They never play on gut reaction. Theirs is a non-emotional game – low on risk or chance. They will memorise the cards and use statistics to calculate possible outcomes. Although they are low-performers, their very logical approach makes them very good at the poker face.

When Analysts are winning

Analysts are unlikely to celebrate although they'll achieve enormous gratification from proving that logic can still be a decisive factor in winning a game that involves chance. Analysts are not impulsive players and so won't take risks just because luck seems to be smiling on them. They may throw their hand in without a moment's hesitation. Because they tend to play statistically there is very little angst in their performance. Expect:

- Little in the way of celebration.
- An appearance of modesty when congratulations are being offered.
- A reining in of gestures or movement. Although the win doesn't cause anxiety it does bring a need for re-focused thinking.
- Staring off to their left. Looking in this direction helps stimulate memory, using calculations to work out the odds of another win.
- A lop-sided smile. Only half the brain will celebrate.

When Analysts are losing

Analysts will beat themselves up when they lose, as they consider it avoidable. Of all the self-blamers, these are the worst because they have least reliance on luck – or lack of it. All displays of emotion will close down. Expect:

- Muttering to themselves.
- Staring at the table rather than at other players or the cards.

- Eye-narrowing.
- OCD-style (swiftly repeated) rituals like finger-tapping or watchstrap-fiddling.
- Quitting.

When Analysts are bluffing

Analysts are good bluffers because they are low-performers at the best of times and therefore difficult to read. This stillness is a natural trait so there will be little in the way of performance or leakage. To spot their bluff, you need to have monitored their smallest movements for patterns over a reasonable space of time. Their core give-aways will be of the type that traditional poker players refer to as 'tells'. These small ritual movements are habitual rather than random and might change between 'winning' and 'losing' rituals.

12

OPPONENTS' BEHAVIOURAL PATTERNS

Good poker players won't wait until they've taken their seats at the table before looking for clues. There are many chances to assess your opponents before the game even starts, such as how they arrive, their pre-game chatter and food/drink ordering, their apparent confidence and their mood. All or any of these can give a useful barometer reading. The aim is to keep in mind the 'bigger picture' in order to build a set of profiles of your opponents.

Poker player Simon Freedman: '*A bluff can be a whole evening thing: how you're offered drinks, whether you sigh or laugh will all be giving information about you. What everyone's trying to do is to get the others to misjudge or miscalculate you.*'

CLOTHING

The way your opponents dress is part of their 'elective' or selected image and as such gives away strong clues about their personality.

These clues will, in turn, give you valuable insights into the way they will play their cards. I've categorised dress styles under a handful of headings. Not everyone you play will fit into these sartorial 'types' but it might give you useful clues if and when they do. Notice, though, that although I use the word 'clues', all we are doing is profile-building. Your opponents' choice of clothing should be placed under the general heading of 'cluster signals', like every other aspect of their non-verbal communication.

Power dressers

Power-dressing involves displays of wealth and/or status. So power dressers might wear designer clothes, expensive watches and sharp suits with padded shoulders.

Poker analysis: Power dressers are highly competitive and driven by the need to win. They'll be wrestling with a desire to win every hand, so expect industrial-strength bluffs. They are already wearing a form of mask so acting out a bluff won't challenge them. They will be good at looking calm under pressure. They'll probably take risks, though, maybe even big ones, although they'll pretend it doesn't hurt when they lose. Expect power dressers to try to undermine your body language by sizing you up. They enjoy staring and smugness as their weapons of mass destruction.

Attention-seeking dressers

Attention seekers choose bright colours, patterns or designs and their hair style and accessories will be chosen to catch the eye. Taste is unimportant. Male attention seekers wear expensive trainers or designer shoes. Females will wear high heels or strappy shoes. They may wear sunglasses indoors, keeping them on for the game or placing them on top of their head.

Poker analysis: They are flashily competitive players, more concerned with image than the power aspect of winning. They will stay in until the end, just to get maximum attention. They will be very likely to bluff and take big risks to do so, as their goal isn't just the pot. They will prefer to overact as a bluff, rather than keep a poker face, which is too understated for their attention-seeking personality. Expect changes in bluff tactics with bluffs, double-bluffs – and, yes, the occasional poker face too, if they feel they're not getting enough attention from the more dramatic routines.

Casually scruffy dressers

Casually scruffy dressers wear clothes that look like they were found in the linen basket that morning. They wear stained or crumpled T-shirts and jeans that have no discernible style or fit.

Poker analysis: Players like this are not forward planners. Their body language signals are often totally lacking in self-awareness so you won't be taking too many risks if you read them at face value. The casually scruffy dresser will often be an impulsive and erratic poker player, working from gut reaction rather than memory or stealth. They have no game-plan and their lack of preparation or focus means your biggest problem will be in finding any pattern in their behaviour. They often play for the hell of it, with food and booze being as much a part of the game as cards and chips.

Scruffy-smart dressers

These players may wear a suit and possibly a tie but they've let the whole outfit go to pot. The suit is crumpled and the trousers shiny. The shirt or blouse is gaping at the buttons. Everything needs a good dry-clean and iron. Their shoes are scuffed and in need of a polish.

Poker analysis: These are characters who are already pretending to be someone they're not. They're only paying lip-service to a smart high-power lifestyle but at heart they're scruffy couch potatoes. They have no real self-control so expect them to play accordingly. They may be low on guilt, so watch for signs of simple bluffing. They're governed by their mood so will be erratic and could be openly stressed. They'll probably take big risks throughout the game. Expect them to learn nothing either. Even if they've been badly burnt in an earlier game they might easily continue to use the same technique again. They'll be capable of bluffing, usually by acting rather than employing a poker face. Their dramatics are rarely well thought out, though, so look for unsubtle signs of leakage.

Smartly casual dressers

These players have turned up looking immaculate but made modifications to their clothes as they've started to play, such as loosening their tie or rolling up their sleeves. They may even change clothes completely, if they've just arrived from work.

Poker analysis: Expect smartly casual players to be ruthless. They're able to sustain a formal, well-groomed look and yet adapt to circumstances. The rolled-up sleeves or loosened tie are symbolic of their ability to change thinking and tactics. When they perform these rituals they're also changing gear and getting down to business. They have a hawk-like focus, concentration and perception. They can switch roles without batting an eyelid and so are very, very likely to bluff. Their ruthless streak means they'll most likely use a poker face technique rather than bothering with histrionics. They can keep this face up for very long periods of time, too.

Casual-obsessive dressers

Never mistake this type for scruffy dressers. Casual-obsessives have a logical and meticulous mind and an eye for detail. They'll remember cards like a computer and play in a logical but successful way. They probably started with online poker, which they excel at. Expect student-style baggy trousers, baggy T-shirts with meaningful logos, non-designer trainers, friendship bands and neck chains.

Poker analysis: Players like this are young and possibly very ruthless. For anyone over the age of 30, casual-obsessives could well be taken for intellectual lightweights with weak playing skills, or geeks or nerds who lack the emotional intelligence to bluff. You could easily be wrong on both counts. These players not only use highly developed logic and have a knack of remembering cards but are brilliant bluffers too. Working on a computer all day has honed their advanced planning skills, desire for world domination and scarily cunning Machiavellian streaks. Underestimate nothing and trust nothing. All that pre-pubescent-looking twitching, gum-chewing and leg-wobbling could easily be part of an act. They're much more methodical than they look, capable of taking very big risks, usually on the final hand when they'll suddenly change gear.

Optimistic dressers

These wear positive and creative colours, such as yellows, oranges and paintbox tones. They look 'at home' in their clothes, without being scruffy. Their garments may have a juvenile look, with cardigans, full, shortish skirts or schoolboy ties in evidence.

Poker analysis: They'll bet in a way that reflects this optimistic streak. They're also quite creative as well and regularly take risks. If they lose they rarely change tactics. Losing for them is only a matter of trying harder next time. Expect a dramatic, risk-taking game that lacks accuracy. Their attention-span is quite low and they're easily distracted by jokes or conversation.

Inappropriate dressers

Inappropriate dressers show a lack of social guilt or responsibility. They just don't fit in. They could well be self-centred and selfish with a distinct lack of empathy or feeling for others. They might even be openly ruthless. They're keen to show that they don't care what others think and are rebellious in their behaviour. They'll wear casual clothes to a smart tournament, gothic to a family game or dress desperately out of season.

Poker analysis: Players like these will dislike the rules, or their opponents, or both. They may have read about tactics and planning and decided to do the opposite. They'll very probably play an emotional and highly charged game because, for them, it's all about knowing better than anyone else. They're unlikely to play to any great game-plan as they prefer to spurn advice and training and prove that a daring amateur can win every time.

Careful dressers

Careful dressers are bland 'fashion-avoiders'. They dress to suit their age and the season and not to look sexy. Colours will be muted and matching or co-ordinating but not heavily so. Shoes will be comfortable rather than fashionable and although they'll never be new they'll be presentable. The smaller details of their clothing will be equally plain but tidy. There will be nothing flash and no designer labels. Their resistance to fashion may look emphatic. If their clothes are formal where others tend to sport casual clothes it should put you on your guard.

Poker analysis: Careful dressers hold very strong values and keep to them stubbornly. Their style of playing is unlikely to change as they are resistant to whim. They will be stubborn players and avoid risk-taking. Expect steady betting but nothing dramatic or impetuous. They'll probably be quiet players, unaffected by the need for 'amateur dramatics'. They'll be good at a poker face, though, as keeping impassive is no problem for them.

EATING AND SMOKING BEHAVIOUR

So what about the way an opponent eats or smokes? Doesn't food and its consumption tell us lots about a player's personality and behaviour? It might not be altogether wholesome to watch people scoffing, smoking or drinking but it can be revealing and I would therefore encourage it.

Players who eat their food quickly and hungrily but without fuss or mess are likely to be ruthless and calculating. Messy, clumsy eaters who gobble down food with their fingers are probably just after a quick buzz and will be sloppy, unplanned players. Noisy eaters who spread out across the table will probably lack any sense of guilt or empathy, and you can expect picky, slow eaters to be tentative, cautious gamblers.

If players smoke, watch to see what they do before lighting up. Do they ask if anyone minds? If so expect their play to be non-devious and non-aggressive. If they just strike up and blow smoke everywhere they'll be ruthless and self-centred in their play. Now watch how they smoke. If they keep tapping at the ash it's probably a sign they're under pressure. If they inhale deeply they have little concern for their own health and well-being so may well be risk-takers at poker.

Smoking also allows you to hear as well as see any changes in your opponent's breathing. Remember the tips about stress levels: negative stress creates shallow and frequent breathing. This can lead to the stressed person gulping in air in sighs or puffing air out to relieve their tension.

If players hold their cigarette in an elegant way, between index and second finger at around the level of their head, they're most probably bluffers – and thespian ones at that. If they hold the cigarette in a stabbing gesture as they tap off the ash they're probably quietly aggressive players. If they hold their index finger across the top of the cigarette as they inhale, or cup the cigarette in their palm, they have strong macho values and probably enjoy playing poker like a cowboy in a saloon.

BODY POSTURE

Always study your opponents' overall posture when they arrive and when they sit down. You can then look for variations and fluctuations. Arrivals are rich pickings for clues about mood and self-esteem.

Negative mood

Someone in a losing or negative mood might:

- Have slumped shoulders.
- Have an annoyed or lost look, glancing around as though unsure they're in the right room.
- Display reduced eye contact or their eyes might scan for drinks or straight to the table.
- Clutch their bag to their body.
- Keep to the edges of the room.
- Go straight to the drinks.

Confidence would send out an opposing set of signals. They might:

- Walk tall.
- Hold their shoulders back and dropped, rather than tense and raised.
- Scan the room with their eyes, looking at faces.
- Display an open, even smile.

Most people have a preferred style of sitting and every move that follows has a linear logic to it. For example, the straight-backed player might lean forward. This is a linear movement. But if he/she suddenly slumps or leans right back this is not a linear movement and you'll know it must therefore be part of a bluff. A naturally slumped player will usually only go from a one-side slump to the other, or vary in their degrees of slump. If they suddenly sit up you should, again, smell a bluff.

If a player leans forward during a game you should expect them to have a strong hand. By leaning forward they're intensifying their focus and displaying a keenness for the game. If their facial expression and other signals are performing a 'bad hand' routine then believe the leaning posture – not the face.

THE HANDSHAKE

How much can you tell from a handshake? Touch is a very powerful communicator and we tend to feel we have the measure of someone the minute we have their palm pressed against our own. But what a beautiful way to start off the first bluff of the evening. Read the handshake but be wary. If your opponents are experienced players and they give you a very weak or a very strong handshake it could well be a personality bluff. Otherwise this is what they usually mean:

- *Dead fish*: Cold, damp and floppy. Almost as though they have no bones in their hand. This would normally signal a weak personality.
- *Bone-crunchers*: Vigorous to the point of inflicting pain, their shake hints that they are determined, competitive, arrogant and ruthless.
- *Sweaty hands*: This could imply nerves or stress but the sweat might have been prompted by social diffidence, not the thought of gambling.
- *Wipers*: They feign thoughtfulness by wiping their hand on their clothes before offering it. Sloppy, non-planners.
- *Fingertip shakers*: They show a lack of enthusiasm for touching that could signal that they are aloof, timid or afraid.

PARALANGUAGE

This is the 'body language of speech', not the words themselves but all those non-linguistic accompaniments such as the pitch or tone of voice, or the pauses between words.

OPPONENTS' BEHAVIOURAL PATTERNS

The hum

Psychologists have noted that it's often not the words we use that convey status and dominance in a group but the 'hum' of the voice, which is often described as timbre. Dominant personalities will sustain their own 'hum' when in conversation with other people. Submissive or subservient people will adapt their own 'hum' to be in keeping with the dominant ones.

When other players are in conversation, keep an ear tuned for this change in 'hum'. Who holds their vocal tone and who drops or raises theirs to fit in? When you hear someone with a sustained tone or hum you can be pretty sure that they have a dominant personality. If so, their play will probably reflect this, making them decisive, ruthless and keen to win at all costs.

If this pattern or tone of hum is at odds with their words, for example if they're performing in a shy, nervous or inexperienced way, you can guess they have a tendency to bluff.

Your opponents' vocal tone will have a subtle but very dramatic effect on your perception of them. You need to be aware of this as the voice is a very easy tool to manipulate. Listen for changes and modulations. It could be a bluff but it could also give you genuine insights if players are less experienced and less aware.

Loud voices

This is a very Alpha sound, especially if the tone is in a lower register. Loud but modulated voices achieve almost instant control of a group, just as higher, breathy voices are seen as passive. A loud voice can be used to control others and dominate the environment. It can also give the impression of extreme confidence. Loud voices smack of egotism as they tend to override other voices, suggesting an 'It's all about me' view of life. Louder voices tend to register impatience, too.

Quiet voices

Quiet voices can belong to someone who is passive, especially if they're hesitant or waffling. But they can also manipulate, by forcing others to listen. If the quieter tone is a change from their normal tone it could be a sign of lying, as speaking quietly is often a sign of trying to 'hide'.

Fast talkers

Naturally fast talkers are quick thinkers and quick decision-takers who will judge a situation speedily. They give the impression of being impulsive and impatient. If a player starts talking quickly when it's not their normal mode of speech it could mean a player is:

- Nervous.
- Anxious.
- Insecure.
- Angry.
- Lying.
- Over-enthusiastic.

Slowed-down speech

Sometimes speech slows down to the point of dumbing-down, giving the impression that players have lost their line of thinking. When the change in rate is sudden it could imply the player is:

- Confused.
- Lying.
- Thoughtful.

Hesitant speech

Hesitant delivery is currently quite popular in politics. Once politicians would show their measure by being assertive and emphatic in delivery. Today, however, politicians often feign measured thoughtfulness to avoid sounding glib and rehearsed. At the poker table, a hesitant delivery may imply that a player is:

- Confused.
- Lying (although look for other signs, such as mouth or face-touching, looking away, tapping or fidgeting).
- Wants to be accurate and is halting to search for the right words (look for focus or concentration signals during pauses).

Breathlessness

Breathlessness or panting can be caused by 'excitement stress' and here's the rub: poker players who want to read another player's body language signals will often put the breathlessness down to the stress of losing. This is rarely true, though. Anxiety signals towards the end of a hand are far more likely to be prompted by a good hand than a bad one. Anticipating a win can produce a much more dramatic effect on the body than fearing they might lose or lying to bluff.

When a player with a good hand is on the brink of winning, their stress signals will often increase dramatically. The excitement and brinkmanship can produce a huge adrenaline rush that the player will try hard to suppress. This can result in short, panting breaths, a higher vocal pitch and even sweating or shaking hands.

13

CLASSIC POKER MOVES

Once you're seated around the table you need to spend every spare moment analysing behaviour patterns and traits. When you're not on a winning hand use this time to judge other players psychologically.

CHIP BEHAVIOUR

It is traditional for poker players to study how opponents handle their chips to glean useful insights into the workings of their brain. On the whole I like this idea but we might need to examine it in a different way from the 'he touched his chips three times so he must have two tens and an ace' kind of way.

People like playing with 'toys' and chips make handy little toys. Even if they're not playing with them you can study the way they've stacked them up or spread them out. The 'toy' factor makes it difficult to change your chip behaviour to bluff your opponents. In many cases what you see is what you get. A tidy perfectionist would find it hard to scatter them carelessly. An untidy player, on the other hand, would struggle to keep them neatly piled.

Bluffing with your chip behaviour would also feel very uncomfortable, almost to the point of bringing bad luck, so I would stick my neck out here and suggest only a very experienced player would bother acting when it comes to placing their chips.

The toy factor affects anyone who is sitting around a table for long periods of time. It is usually completely unselfconscious and is therefore very telling. When I run training courses the bowl of sweets or the pens or even the Blu-tac become toys.

When the delegates leave the room they leave amazing personality tracks via their 'toy' debris. Some are hoarders, some make designs or patterns, some stack and others just turn things into rubbish. We're the same at the dinner table. Once most of the food is eaten see how diners begin to convert anything close to hand into toys. The wax from candles is popular, so are foil wrappers, unused cutlery or napkins.

All this semi-compulsive behaviour can give clues about a person's state of mind or character, so build chip behaviour into your overall player profile.

The stacker

If players stack their chips, look for patterns in the stacking. How neat are the piles? Do they straighten and re-straighten them as a comfort gesture? If players are using compulsive neatness, keeping all stacks the same height and touching them to keep them in order, we can assume they're perfectionists who prefer order to chaos.

This behaviour is common in sport. When players are concerned with detail you'll know they're focused and careful and possibly very disciplined and work hard at their game. They probably lack natural talent or even luck but compensate with diligence and preparation. Expect them to be first-class players.

This kind of orderly thinking gives them reassurance. They're often seen as non-risk-takers and, in a way, that's true – but don't expect them to be over-careful either.

They might not take risks for the sake of it but their methodical play will wear you down and they'll happily make daring decisions based on planning rather than gut reaction. They're very likely to bluff. They're skilled at managing their own emotions and turning them to their own benefit. They'll probably display bravery and coolness under pressure. They might even use one or two intimidation tactics.

They'll avoid high drama though, preferring to poker-face. They can keep this face in place for long periods of time. For them, it is seen as a professional demeanour.

The chip-fondler

Some players toy with their chips, picking up the piles and letting them drop one at a time, or fingering the stacks, or tapping with them. These players find gambling sexy. The game, the risk, the winning are all a huge turn-on for them. They'll rarely be interested in safe sex. They enjoy getting their kicks and will take risks to heighten the tension. Expect them to play above their means or close to it and to make very daring, spur-of-the-moment decisions. Players like these know no fear but might be clever players too, so don't underestimate them just because they appear reckless. Avoid getting into a bidding war unless you're convinced you have the better hand.

The chip-tapper

Tapping is a metronomic gesture of impatience, self-stimulation or self-calm. Expect tappers to be edgy and nervous. They may like to play quickly and get frustrated waiting for their turn. If the tapping is constant then this is their natural personality. But if it's sporadic keep a close eye on it. Do they suddenly become impatient when they have a good hand? Are they eager to win? Or do they tap when they're losing and just about to fold? Their impatience might lead to reckless calls. Note the speed of the tapping too. Fast means stressed and impatient, slow can signal they're keeping their emotions in check.

The chip-splayer

Stacking indicates methodical play, so the opposite, splaying the chips, shows a lack of method and a reckless view of money. Splayers take risks and tend to suffer as they play. If they're equally unstructured in their other habits, for example spreading food around their plate or eating with greasy fingers, they want instant gratification and live for the moment without concern for the consequences. This attitude can easily infect their poker. Their head will be full of internal dialogues and they'll go with the one that shouts loudest. They'll be happy to sit on a bad hand and bluff it out, right to the end. No doubt they think this is what poker's all about. Their body language bluffing skills are basic, though, because they have little game-play.

The chip-gazer

Chip-gazers study their chips. Some glance quickly; others maintain a steady gaze. The steady chip-gazer is possibly money-focused and worried about losing. They're staring to calculate and because they're staring directly at their chips the calculation is probably gloomy – they're working out how much they can afford to lose. If they're visualising winning with a good hand then they'll be more likely to stare at your chips with the thought that your money will soon be theirs.

Some degree of chip-watching is natural. Indeed, there are times when it just wouldn't be natural to look away from them, for example when they're being handed out or pushed across. At these moments chips are like foodstuff as far as the brain and eyes are concerned and it's almost impossible not to look. If you don't believe me, try this test. Next time you're in a restaurant, try not to stare at the food as it's being served.

So players who *don't* stare at their chips when they change hands are fighting the impulse for a reason. That's probably because they're bluffing. When players are dealt their hand and glance quickly at their chips they probably have a good hand. This tends to be an optimistic glance rather than a gloomy one.

PLACING A BET

Many theories have been written about the way players place their bets. From the throwers and hurlers to the sliders or the slow and reluctant inchers, you can be sure that the method of moving chips will leak out some clues about the state of their hand. But beware of doing an on-the-spot analysis based on this one gesture, and consider habits and patterns as well.

Watch to see your opponents' normal way of moving their chips. Then look for irregularities. Do they throw the chips sometimes and push the pile at other times? Can you attach any patterns to their previous hands? If they throw their chips when the hand is good and slide them slowly when it's bad then you're onto a winner.

But also consider their level of experience and downright craftiness. Are they likely to be bluffers and clever ones at that? Could they be setting you up for a fall? Is it possible that they have been carefully creating this pattern for you and the other players in the knowledge that breaking it on a key hand could give them an 'easy' win? Are you being fooled?

If you are then you must be playing a strategist not an 'instant gratification' player. Scamming like this can take time and also blast much of the 'fun' element out of the game. Do they seem 'delayed gratification' types? Do they ever celebrate a win or display anger or upset when they lose? Are they quiet and low-key? If so this could all fit the strategist profile, so – be afraid, be very afraid . . .

Always remember the golden rules of body language: first look for the 'performed' signals – the biggest display gestures. Then study the subtle 'leakage' gestures. Do they add up? Are they congruent? If not, then assume the 'performed' gestures are just that – a performance to bluff opponents. Assume the exact opposite to be true.

They might peek at their cards and give a facial 'performance' of displeasure. But then you glance down and see the thumbs are erect or there's a happy little leg-tap going on beneath the table. In that case it might be safe to assume the hand is strong, not weak. On the other hand, the facial performance could include lip-licking, smiling or a quick eyebrow-raise. But you also notice that the shoulders have slumped, or an increase of self-comfort gestures such as hair-stroking or nail-fiddling. In this case you can safely assume the hand isn't as good as the facial expression is telling you.

Watch the way your opponents move their chips as they bet. Do they push them across smoothly or throw them about randomly? Smooth movers are likely to be analytical and careful players. If they're betting big then they probably have a good hand. Chip-tossers are far more casual about their money and the bet. Chip-tossing is unsubtle and even noisy, suggesting they'll probably be risk-takers and impulsive gamblers.

Sullen betters may be acting sulky to imply a bad hand. Now watch the action and decide what they're trying to tell you. If they're dismissive and angry they're trying to say their luck is bad and it's 'doing their head in'. Unless they're very stupid players this can't be true. If they're still betting they wouldn't risk money by signalling so obviously, so assume they're bluffing. As with all signs of 'leakage', though, study chip-moving behaviour as early in the game as possible. Then you can look for variations and know what they mean.

SHOWING THE CARDS

I always thought the need to show off your cards to a non-player was a very British trait. But it seems they do it in the USA too. Sharing the information with a non-playing friend or partner shows a desire to double the fun. I have heard it suggested that players only let others see their cards if the hand is good, but the opposite is more likely to be true in the UK. Very few British players would flaunt a good hand. We're more likely to gain empathy by displaying a truly awful hand that we're bluffing with and asking the friend to help us with the bluff.

So . . . watch the friends. They'll be put on the spot but keen to join in the fun. A double-bluff is highly unlikely in case it is read as an honest response that gives the hand away. Similarly, they're unlikely to be honest so assume they'll join in the bluff. Expect their acting to be less subtle. See their reaction and feel relatively safe assuming the opposite is true.

STAYING CALM

Calmness is a peculiar quality. Few people feel genuinely calm while playing poker. In fact many play for the adrenaline rush poker gives them so it seems pointless to play the game if you feel calm about it. Poker is exciting. So who would be really calm? For a player to be completely calm playing poker there are probably only one of two options:

- They're new, bored, you're playing for mints and they hate sweets.
- They're very experienced to the point where nothing fazes them. So why play poker? For money. This can be the only answer. But even if the game doesn't make them excited, surely the amount in the pot should, if money is their key motivation? The only explanation must be that they've played it for years and don't need the cash.

LOOKING AT A HAND

Peeking at a hand should be a grade-A piece of leakage but in fact it is unreliable. Peeking looks dramatic but the reasons for peeking are varied and often random. If we think in a linear fashion, someone who peeks must have forgotten their cards. More cards have been dealt and they need to remind themselves of what they already hold. This should imply that their hand is not exciting or it would be in their memory.

However . . . it is possible they have an exciting hand and like to keep looking at it. Many people enjoy peeking even when they know what's there. Peeking is life-enhancing. So never assume it means your opponent has a weak hand.

Some people peek as part of their playing ritual. They peek to think or peek to create time. They peek even though they know what's there, just as commuters look at the destination board more than once when running to catch a train. It's a nervous ritual, and implies anxiety rather than information-gathering. Check whether peekers are habitual or occasional. Infrequent peeking could be leakage so study their peeking behaviour to see whether they do it on a winning or losing hand.

Peeking can give the false impression that they need to remind themselves of their hand – and can be a bluff. Their expression will be one of evaluation, as though deciding whether or not to take a risk.

If experienced opponents check or double-check their cards you should be suspicious of the time spent looking. If you need to double-check, the second look need only ever be a glance. You're doing just that – checking. So if your opponent double-checks and the second glance becomes extended, suspect a bluff.

PROTECTING THE HAND

Players who protect their cards will usually have a strong hand. If they hold them close to the chest or keep them flat on the table with fingers on top you can guess they're good, especially the chest-clutch ones. Rarely do we pull something close to our bosom if we don't like it.

FLASHERS

Every once in a while you'll play with a card-flasher. These are players who 'accidentally' let you see a card, or even a couple, while they play. Now this can, of course, be mere clumsiness. However, clumsiness generally only occurs with inexperienced or 'don't care' players. Everyone else guards their hands. So what does flashing from experienced players tell you? They could be drunk, although good players will normally stay sober. Otherwise, if this is a bluff, assume that a high-card flash means a weak hand and a low-card flash means a strong one.

PRE-EMPTIVE STRIKES

A childish but potentially effective body language technique is to give the impression that you can't wait to place a bet. To do this, players produce what is called an 'intentional gesture' – staring at the player betting while holding your own chips raised, waiting to strike. There's no subtlety in this routine and it would rarely – if ever – be anything but a bluff. Its aim is to change your betting behaviour by implying they have a gem of a hand. It's supposed to intimidate you into backing down. But because it puts pressure on you it can still be a potent piece of gamesmanship.

It's not going to be accidental as players know they're giving too much away with the gesture. So it must be deceptive. But in what way? Do they have a lousy hand and want to fool you into thinking it's good? Or is this a double-scam? Is their hand good and they're hoping you'll think it's bad and bet accordingly? Much of the truth will come out via the player's facial expression. If it's a single scam and they have a bad hand they'll probably feel inclined to laugh as their attempt to deceive is so clumsy. If it's a double-scam they'll probably keep a straight face.

STARING

Research at Newcastle University suggests that having a pair of staring eyes fixed on us encourages us to be honest. A poster was placed above an honesty box and almost three times as much money was placed in the box when the poster featured a pair of staring eyes as when it showed a bunch of flowers. So how can we use this playing poker? Be unafraid. When opponents seem to be bluffing simply stare at them. This may go against your upbringing but do it. They are under greater pressure to be honest and so more likely to give away some clues that could work in your favour.

If a player stares at you while you're making your bet you could assume they're holding a weak hand and trying to intimidate you by looking strong. However they could also be holding a strong hand and looking at what they see as their winnings. You can see quite easily which option it is. In the first case the player will be staring at your face, trying to inhibit your body language signals. In the second the player will be looking primarily at your chips. Remember, the two are entirely different.

INTENTIONAL GESTURE BLUFFS

Intentional bluffers pretend to perform an action too early as a 'mistake'. For instance they might start to spread a winning hand before it's their turn. This 'mistake' is to bluff you into thinking they've let the cat out of the bag, which of course they haven't. But it can easily affect your own betting decision.

An example of the 'intentional gesture' is the 'High Noon' routine. This can occur when you're about to bet and an opponent decides to put you off betting by giving the impression they have a strong hand. They do this by miming impatience and eagerness to place their own bet. The High Noon player is very likely to perform any or all of the following as you're about to bet:

- Staring.
- Fingering their chips.
- Beginning to push their chips across.
- Tapping or other impatience gestures – but combined with eye contact.
- Leaning forward looking ready to strike.

This will be a bluff if you see it in any but the least experienced players. They're bluffing by pretending they have a strong hand, so expect the opposite.

A player may also display the exact opposite signals as you deliberate over your bet. This means they will look uninterested or even bored, pretending to have a weak hand that's not worth bothering with. If this happens, expect:

- Yawning.
- Looking away.
- Whistling or humming.
- Tapping with no eye contact.
- Folded arms.
- Sitting back in the seat.

Again, if these occur just as you consider your bet, this player could be bluffing which means they have a strong hand and are pretending that it's so weak it's hardly worth bothering with.

BLUFFING A BET

The key bluffing opportunities occur, of course, when it's time to place the bets. This is the bluffer's performance moment. Do they try to appear weak and negative or strong and bullish? Do they shrug and puff and squirm a little? Do they wince slightly in pain as they push their chips? Does their chip-pushing look weak and reluctant? Then expect them to be bluffing and holding a strong hand.

They might appear indecisive as they place their bet. Their head will tilt sideways. They'll begin to push the chips then change their mind. They might even remove a few chips from the pile. If their desire is to make you feel safe about placing your own bet then they'll keep these gestures low-key to avoid alerting you. Once they've placed their bet they will probably become quite still.

Alternatively . . . do they bang the chips down confidently or even throw them into the pot? Do they bet quickly and with authority? Are they smiling as they place their bet? Would you describe their demeanour as slightly victorious? Then you should guess they have a weak hand as they're bluffing in a way to pretend they have a strong one.

Bluffing a win

This will occur while players are making their bet and the bluffer starts to mime the first few moves of picking up the pot. It's as though they've already won. They might extend their arms towards the pot in an 'embrace' or sweeping movement. Or it might be just one hand. They might lean forward suddenly towards the pot and even lift their bottom a little way off the seat.

The idea, of course, is to make you think their hand is so strong that they've as good as won already. This form of 'intentional gesture' sounds so obvious, you might think you'd never be suckered – but in a tense moment it can work, if they bluff well enough and the timing is right. Just remember that if they're trying to tell you they have a very strong winning hand then – as usual – expect the opposite to be true.

PEEKING AT YOU

We've already established that whole-body acting is hard. When opponents feign lack of interest as you're deciding on your bet, take a moment to look at their eyes. They'll be drawn towards you, your cards and your chips like a fly's drawn to jam. If their head is turned away slightly and – when you look up – you see their eyes pointing in your direction, assume the turn of the head is a bluff. They're trying to look as though they have no interest in your hand because their own is so indifferent. Which means it isn't, of course. But the eyes are the 'leakage' you're looking for. They will tell you about their true intentions and levels of interest.

NOISES OFF

A bluff can be aural as well as visual. We've already established that it's easier to lie using words than it is using body language, and lying via sounds is a close relative to speaking. When players are studying their hands they may find it easier – and more useful – to make a noise-bluff than a body-bluff. Here are some common sound-bluffs.

Sighing

This will usually be performed as the player first looks at his/her cards or is about to place a bet. A sigh is a sound of regret. They're trying to make you think they have a weak hand and are saying goodbye to their cash. If this is a bluff then assume their hand is strong.

Puffing

Puffing is a release of tension. If it's genuine it can mean a strong hand. If it's a bluff it means the bluffer is trying to imply they have a weak hand that is worrying them and making them anxious. Assume they have the opposite.

Tutting

This is a small noise with an enormous impact. It is the quickest and easiest signal of disapproval that there is. Modern manners are kept in line by the power of the 'tut'. We 'tut' when we see something we dislike, possibly intensely. But it is very rarely instinctive. It's a full-blown conversational device, albeit a very lazy one, and is intended to be heard by an audience. The intention of a real 'tut' is to register complaint and enlist others into agreeing with you or sympathising with your plight.

When you 'tut' to yourself you're letting everyone know you're annoyed, often with the fate the gods have dealt you. So in poker this is intended to imply that players are disappointed with cards they've been dealt. Assume they have a strong hand. If a player tuts as you make a move they're probably trying to let you know that you've just scuppered their game, so assume they're strong. Of course, it could mean you've breached etiquette in some way. So analyse your own behaviour first. Otherwise assume the tutting player is bluffing.

STRESS LEAKAGE

It's easy to assume the worst symptoms of stress will emerge when you're losing and that if your opponents' hands start shaking or they start to get twitchy then they're heading for a big loss. But this assumption can lose you money, too.

Firstly, look at the psychological process. You're watching England in the World Cup and they are 3–0 down. How are you behaving? Shaking with nerves or anxiety? Fidgeting? Full of sudden energy? No, you're slumped, physically relaxed, depressed, possibly sloping off out of the ground. Any action seems beyond your energies and your ability to speak has diminished. When you do talk your vocal tone has dropped and your speech slowed down.

Most people don't like losing but they're no stranger to the feeling. The experience of losing is one we recall and retain for our entire lives. Even optimists suffer from this. When you win something important it rarely prompts feelings of *déjà vu*, but lose and all the previous losses in your life come back to haunt you. None of this provokes physical symptoms of stress.

The stress response at cards is much more likely to be associated with winning. Now imagine England are 2–1 up in the World Cup and there's ten minutes of the game to go. What are you doing? Smiling and laughing as you contemplate success? No, you're half mad with anxiety and it will build until the final whistle's blown. Even if Rooney gets another ball into the net and the lead becomes more comfortable the tension in your body will be unbearable.

It's often the proximity to the big win that causes the shakes. Assuming the poor guy with the shaking hands is about to lose his shirt could leave you slaughtered. Even if the keys to his Porsche are lying on the table he's much more likely to be suffering a different emotion if he's gambling his car on a very weak hand. If he's into taking risks that size he's an adrenaline junkie anyway and one more burst won't fire him up as much as a player on the brink of a big win.

So how do you use the stressful effects of a winning hand? Stress releases adrenaline and causes muscle tension, shallow, panting breaths, a raised vocal tone, dry mouth and accelerated heart beat. Think you can spot those in your opponent? So . . . first look for the stress signal, small though it may be. We're less used to the more pleasurable emotions and therefore less able to mask them, like:

- The quick intake of breath.
- The slight shudder of the shoulders.
- The tightening of the shoulder muscles.
- The shaking hands.
- The big swallow.

And then there are the total pleasure signals like:

- Licking the side of the mouth.
- Straightening of the back.
- The pupil dilation.
- Leg pumping.

A classic men-only habit is the erect thumbs – this always signals pleasure. Watch David Beckham or Joe Cole come onto the pitch when they're looking forward to a game. They run across the ground with their hands high on their chests and their thumbs sticking upward. Shayne Ward did the same thing when he ran onto the stage during the heats and finals of *The X Factor* (which he won). Tony Blair sports erect thumbs during Prime Minister's Question Time, when he is on top of the questions and able to answer them confidently.

Now most of these signals of pleasure will occur as soon as the winning hand has been spotted. Some of them, like pupil dilation and the subtle intake of breath, are spontaneous and instant. It's all the player can do to stop themselves from jumping onto their chair and punching the air. So you need to watch as the cards are dealt and glanced at for the first time. The longer it takes for the pleasure micro-gestures to appear, the more you can guess that they're being manufactured.

Bear in mind, though, that your opponent might just be slow at reading the cards or a newcomer is trying to remember what constitutes a winning hand. Or they could be numerically dyslexic, like me. I need to count on my fingers or say the numbers out loud. With players like this you might see a slow build-up of realisation. With more experienced players you should see something a whole lot more speedy.

THE LEG PUMP AND LEG SWING

The leg pump is another men-only signal of pleasure. With some men it's almost non-stop and I have met guys who do it with both legs at once. Leg-pumping is a happy sign. Women rarely do the leg pump but may employ the leg swing, sitting with legs crossed and swinging the top leg from the knee down. This is rarely a sign of pleasure and far more likely to indicate suppressed irritation, anger or impatience.

14

ANALYSIS OF YOUR OPPONENTS' BODY GESTURES

Now we're going to go into close-up, working through all those body language variables and giving them an open-minded analysis. This is your beginner's guide to spotting bluffs via leakage 'clues'.

THINKING

When you see 'thinking signals' you can assume your opponent has a mediocre hand. If they had a good hand they wouldn't be thinking. Thinking is usually acted out via body language in an almost exaggerated way. Why? Well it requires a pause in the action and pauses we cause make us nervous. We're holding other people up for what appears no good reason. So we feel the need to explain by way of apology.

In many ways it's similar to the non-verbal etiquette we employ during other 'waiting' moments in our lives. People get impatient or angry when we make them wait so we feel obliged to act out what we're doing. If you're holding up the traffic while deciding which route to take you'll wave and shrug to indicate your dilemma.

If you're holding up a queue you'll gesture both reason and apologies so as not to bear the brunt of other people's anger. The impetus to gesticulate when you pause to think around a poker table is strong. Players who are genuinely thinking will:

- Gaze into the middle distance.
- Gaze at the floor.
- Stick out their tongue.
- Pull in their lips.
- Look up and to the left for recalled memory.
- Look up and to the right for creative or imaginative thought.
- Cover their face with their hands.
- Rub the back of their head.
- Cover their ears.

Acted thinking is intended to show what's going on and apologise for the pause. It has little to do with genuine thought-stimulation and is more of a polite ritual of signalled mime. Acted thinking would include:

- Narrowing the eyes.
- Puffing.
- Tilting the head.
- Staring at the cards.
- Tapping the mouth or face.
- Taking a deep breath in and letting it out slowly.
- Putting the fingers over the mouth.

- Scratching the side of the head.
- Making 'thinking noises'.
- Stuffing fingers into the mouth.
- Puckering up the lips.
- Humming.
- Leaning back in the chair.

While there are differences in what prompts either the genuine thinking signals or the acted ones, the message is the same: if there is a need to think there is no clear-cut decision. Once you consider this then it will be an invaluable piece of leakage as the cards are turning. Ask yourself what thinking might say about the cards already dealt. If it is a good hand there would be little need for a thinking pause. If the dealt card is a good one but the player still stops to think you have good information about the other cards they're holding.

Suppose your opponent calls without pausing to think. In that case any changes in that behaviour after the cards have been dealt should give you a guide to their hand. If they pause to think after a good card has been dealt you can assume it hasn't helped the hand. This in turn should give you a guide as to what their hand contains. If they'd called without thinking before and the new card had improved the hand then you could assume they'd call without thinking again. If they pause you could assume the card hasn't improved the hand.

ANXIETY

As we discussed in Chapter 6, the autonomic nervous system controls our states of action and relaxation.

- The *sympathetic* nervous system controls high activity and high stimulation.
- The *parasympathetic* nervous system controls low activity and low stimulation.

So how does this affect your opponent? Well, when players are bluffing they'll be in a state of high activity, with the sympathetic nervous system gearing up for flight or fight. If they're bluffing they'll be struggling to mask all the symptoms of this state. When the sympathetic system kicks in, so does the adrenaline, and this produces visual symptoms.

With their parasympathetic system in conflict with their sympathetic they'll find it difficult to sit still and act calm. Several visual clues might be hard to mask and you should look for any or all of these tell-tale signs:

- The posture is controllable and might even be relaxed but masking breathing takes a lot of practice. If opponents are sitting in a relaxed pose but their chest is rising and falling quickly you can assume they're bluffing and only pretending to be cool.
- Skin pallor is a symptom of the sympathetic nervous system response. This is almost impossible to mask.
- The mouth dries, making movements with the tongue and lips more frequent. When David Cameron became Tory leader and was interviewed by Jeremy Paxman for the first time he maintained a calm expression and vocal tone but his lip-licking, tongue-poking and lip-pursing gestures increased dramatically.
- The body is itching for activity, but this is impossible. So players often compensate by using 'clamped-limb' gestures,

such as tightly crossed legs, or one hand may press the other down to keep it still.

If the battle between sympathetic and parasympathetic symptoms increases you may see intense fluctuations that bluffers struggle to mask. During periods of intense pressure, when we're unable to display our pressure symptoms, we often swing back and forth like a pendulum. This could produce:

- A blush or nervous rash on the neck, which replaces pallor.
- Excessive salivation lubricating a previously dry mouth.
- A sudden urge to visit the loo, indicated by tightly crossed legs.

CUT-OFFS

Cut-offs are eye movements caused by an impulsive need to 'take a break' from a transaction. This can be prompted by anxiety, stress, or guilt at bluffing. Because the eyes are hard to control without over-compensating and hard staring, it's always worth asking opponents a question when you think they're trying to perform a bluff. Their eye movement as they answer could give you a clue to their state of mind. There are four key types of eye cut-offs:

- *Shifty eyes*: Players glance away and then back to you. This is so well-documented in the annuls of lying body language that you'll probably only see it from players who are new to bluffing.
- *Evasive eyes*: Here, players prefer to avoid all eye contact with you and look into the distance instead.

- *Stammering eyes*: Players look at you but unconsciously want to close their eyelids to avoid looking and so blinking is prolonged.
- *Stuttering eyes*: Here the blink-rate is accelerated or erratic.

DISPLACEMENT ACTIVITIES

Whether players are winning or losing, when they try to bluff their masked emotions can leak out through displacement activities. This is a delayed version of the true emotion or reaction and can be very telling. Some bluffers think that if the action isn't performed as a direct result of the cards then the other players won't smell a rat. So this won't appear at the moment of anger/anxiety but will usually occur during a 'safe' time, such as when another player is making a decision.

Displacements might be due to re-directed anger or frustration/anxiety at a bad hand, which can lead to:

- Scratching.
- Tapping.
- Flicking chips.
- Foot-stamping.
- Throwing small items.
- Nail-biting.
- Folding handkerchiefs, napkins and so on.

Alternatively, displacements might indicate displaced joy at a good hand. This will normally emerge with the excuse of speaking to another player or friend and over-smiling or laughing.

PUPIL CHANGES

Pupil size is primarily affected by changes in light levels. The pupils shrink to pinhead size in bright light and enlarge in a dark room. But these responses are also prompted by emotion and are impossible to mask except with sunglasses.

When we see something pleasurable or exciting our pupils expand automatically. If you spot this reaction in an opponent just after they've been studying their cards you can assume they have a very good hand. When we see something we dislike our pupils contract. So pinpoint pupils will probably signal a very bad hand.

HANDS

When you look at the main performance gestures, such as smiling, anger, impatience or poker face, most of these are acted out on the face and torso. Now compare the signals you're being sold with the hand movements. Look for discrepancies. If the hands are saying something in direct contrast to the face or body, believe the hands are giving the genuine message.

EYE BEHAVIOUR

The eyes reveal so much about our thinking and feelings that tournament players often pitch up in sunglasses or visors. Personally I would ban any eye-covering bigger than false eyelashes or heavy mascara. Avoid props like these yourself as you'll look pretentious. Wearing them at friendly or amateur games is especially pointless. It announces that you think you're a top player and that you're going to play mind games. This puts everyone on their guard immediately. Much better to look honest and a little stupid.

Steely gaze

If your opponent has you locked in an industrial-strength stare you need to keep in mind that this is not natural body language. Nobody in the real world enjoys this kind of eye-combat. It makes the starer look aggressive or in love. So, staring in this intense way just has to be a bluff. It's an unnatural act. Okay, it's a sign of strength but it's a sign of body language strength, not card strength.

Sideways glance

When opponents think they have a chance of taking the pot they'll feel an urge to estimate how well the remaining players are likely to play. They'll want to guess who'll fold, which means they'll probably spend time glancing or even looking towards the players to their left.

SIGNS OF THINKING

In everyday situations we show we are thinking in certain subtle ways. In poker these 'thinking signs' can reveal clues about your opponents' state of mind, especially if they are bluffing.

Tilted head = subtle thoughtfulness

This gesture indicates decisive thinking. In conversation we do it to show we are paying close attention to the speaker. If a player is just pondering over their hand you can assume they have a medium hand, rather than a good one. It's quite a happy thinking gesture so the hand is unlikely to be very bad.

Bluffing: If the head-tilt is a bluff then the hand is likely to be very good as this player is acting out a 'thinking' gesture, which can only mean they don't have to consider at all. The head-tilt might be too subtle and they could add a finger over the lips or a bottom-lip-shrug gesture to complete the performance.

Staring at cards or into the distance = concentration or memory access

The eyes move in the direction that will stimulate the appropriate part of the brain. If players are studying their cards for a long time they're thinking hard. This should give you clues as to the state of their hand. Gazing into the distance is a different type of thinking, though. The upper middle means accessing stored knowledge so they could be trying to remember tactics. If they've been staring into the distance for a long time their thoughts are less logical. They could be working out how much money they can afford to gamble and what it would mean to their bank balance.

Bluffing: If staring at their cards is a bluff you can assume it is being performed to help keep the poker face in place. Looking down at the cards means avoiding give-away emotional signals from the eyes. Players like this are signalling that they no longer need to read the other players, otherwise they'd be looking around. This could suggest the hand is either spectacularly good or very bad.

Looking up to their right = creative thinking

This is a sign that they are accessing the imaginative side of the brain. These players have gone 'off-piste' logic-wise. They could be seeing how much they might get away with when they bluff and how to bluff. Alternatively they *could* be imagining how they'll spend their winnings although this is highly unlikely as – if their hand is that good – they should still be focusing on the game.

Bluffing: This movement is so instinctive it is rarely used as a bluff. As it has a genuine effect on thinking style it could ruin a player's game.

Looking up to their left = logical thinking

In this case players are normally accessing the logical side of the brain and so are still tuned in and thinking of the mathematics of the cards themselves or the statistical chances of winning. They are also delving into recalled memory so could be trying to remember which cards have been dealt and when. This could mean you're playing with a human computer. This player is still very much in there so avoid making any risky or rash decisions.

Bluffing: This movement is so instinctive it is rarely used as a bluff. As it has a genuine effect on thinking style it could ruin a player's game.

Looking slightly down = internal dialogue

This will usually be a sign that the player is having a conversation with him/herself. If you want to be polite you should let this conversation continue to enable them to work out their next steps. If you want to play mean, interrupt the flow by coughing, tapping or even speaking to them.

Bluffing: This movement is so instinctive it is rarely used as a bluff. As it has a genuine effect on thinking style it could ruin a player's game.

ANALYSIS OF YOUR OPPONENTS' BODY GESTURES

Stilled thinking = poised to strike

If players suddenly become very still while thinking they are probably poised to strike, especially if there is tension in their pose. Look for a very subtle acceleration in breathing to confirm this. This could be deep thinking or waiting. If their hand is bad there could be a suggestion of 'exit' going on: a slightly slumped posture, or eyes darting from the area of play or a slowing down in breathing.

Bluffing: Stillness is the classic poker face bluff. Your opponents could be stopping all movement to perform the lie. Some people like to act their lie while others prefer to use stillness to mask all emotions. If your opponent is in permanent poker face mode from arrival to departure you're going to have very little in the way of clues to go on and you'll need to be searching for patterns in breathing, eye movement, or whatever movements they do have to perform, such as pushing their chips. If they're intermittent poker face players, only putting it in place during key moments in the action, you will at least have a guide to their tactics.

Chewing lip or pen = focused thinking

Lip-chewing, like poking your tongue out, is a common attention-intensifier, used to focus our thoughts and help us to concentrate. Chewing while thinking is a classic self-comfort gesture. It should suggest to you that your opponents are feeling anxious, and give you some idea of the state of their hand. Lip or pen-chewing is an echo gesture, copying the act of breast-feeding as a baby in an effort to self-calm. Sometimes this gesture can be quite dramatic, with the fingers pushing the lower lip into the mouth. This will rarely if ever be performed over a strong hand.

Bluffing: Lip-chewing is an unsubtle bluff that should immediately give away the fact that the player has a good hand. If they're an accomplished actor they'll tone the gesture down a notch for subtlety, skewing slightly pursed lips to one side instead.

Head-scratching = mulling over decision

Head-scratching tends to be employed only in emergency situations, when the scratcher is truly puzzled. This is a signal of mild confusion, especially if the scratching takes place around the back of the head.

Bluffing: As a bluff, the head scratch is another acted gesture that lacks subtlety. I would expect the bluffing head-scratcher to add to the performance by shaking their head at the same time. They might also sigh. I think this should be enough for you to know that they're sitting on a good hand and trying to pretend it's bad.

Leaning back in chair = long-term thinking

Here players have, in effect, removed themselves from the game to devote more time to their thinking. By taking themselves away from the action they're signalling a need for a clear head with less distraction.

Bluffing: As a bluff, sitting away from the table is usually performed to signal sulking, as in 'this hand is so bad I'm not playing'. Obviously the bluffer is actually thinking the opposite. An over-performing bluffer might add to the 'throwing the toys out of the pram' routine by throwing the cards down or puffing.

SIGNS OF BOREDOM

True boredom can be indicated by many different signs, such as:

- Sighing.
- Glancing at watch.
- Doodling.
- Shifting in the seat.
- Metronomic gestures, such as tapping.
- Stretching.
- Rolling eyes.
- Resting chin on palm of hand.
- Picking at nails.

In an inexperienced player, you could take the gesture at face value. If they've lost interest in the game then they probably aren't winning. If it's one of their first few games they could be turned off by the game of poker altogether, winning or not. Whatever the reason, you can assume they're not really focused on the game. Which means they're unlikely to even be thinking about bluffing. If you're not playing for money you can be pretty sure they'll only win if their hand is exceptionally good.

Bluffing: Why would any player choose boredom as their bluff? The more obvious options if you have an excellent hand would be regret, sadness or irritation at the cards. Boredom is a stagnant state to act as a bluff. It is on nodding terms with impatience, so could easily look as though you can't wait for the game to move on, which could signal you're close to winning. Boredom is a hard bluff to pull off if they have a good hand as they will be playing against instinct. So, if subtle, expect this bluff to come from an experienced bluffer. If it lacks subtlety, though, employing several of the above, you can be sure they have a good hand.

SIGNS OF FRUSTRATION

Grimacing

Wincing or grimacing as you're dealt your cards is an instinctive response to gain pity or sympathy from other players. In a very inexperienced player it could be taken at face value, which means they have a poor hand. Of course no experienced player would allow this knee-jerk reaction as it gives too much away so you would automatically assume it's a bluff. But then, a grimace is such a simple and obvious bluff that it could be a double-bluff. So where does this take us? A single-bluff grimace will be aimed at convincing you their good hand is a bad one, so a double-bluff grimace is performed to convince you they're pretending their bad hand is a bad one from which they want you to assume it's actually a good one. (Phew!)

Shrugging

An inadvertent shrug signals both frustration at a poor hand and also fatalism – the acceptance of a run of bad luck. In many ways it says, 'That was all I was expecting.' This makes it quite a complex gesture and so an unlikely choice for a bluff as the brain has to juggle two meanings that are opposed to reality. So – if you see inexperienced players shrug the chances are they really are unimpressed with their hand. At best it could be workable, but not impressive. It would be an unusual gesture for an experienced player – except as a bluff – but not unknown.

Bluffing: Indifference as a bluff can only mean the exact opposite. So, if they're trying to act nonchalant by shrugging it means their hand must be spectacular. Your problem is, spectacularly bad or spectacularly good? Look at their mouth for a clue. If the hand is good they may overact and throw in a 'mouth shrug' as well.

Hands on top of the head

This is a sign that things are getting out of control. If genuine it implies the player is having an emphatic run of bad luck, and can hardly believe it. In many ways it's a gesture of 'holding your head on' and signals despair.

Bluffing: If it's a bluff, it's overacted and would only come from players who think their bluffing is better than it is. Expect it to be a very basic bluff and assume their hand is strong.

Hands behind head

This is what's called pit-baring. It's a gesture of arrogance, smugness and a belief that they feel superior to their opponents. They're letting you know they think you're a pushover. If they sit back in their seat to do it they're truly emphasising their point.

Bluffing: Now, the question is, why would a player want to signal 'smug'? The only answer is that it's a bluff and they're keen to undermine your confidence. There could really only be one reason why they want to let you know that they're going to win and it's that they're not sure they are. They're going for the 'ripple effect', trying to get you to change the way you play. They're probably sitting on a medium to good hand, hoping to boost it by getting you to drop out. Of course the easy answer is to refuse to be undermined by this behaviour. If it's what they want then don't do it. Play with confidence. Ignore them.

Eye-closing

This is a very dramatic barrier gesture. It shuts us off instantly and totally from the rest of the room in a way that arm-folding or leg-crossing can never achieve. When we close our eyes we tend to gain instant attention from everyone around us. It will usually prompt concern from other people, too. If inexperienced players close their eyes the second they glance at their cards they're signalling that they don't like what they see. In effect, they are saying, 'I'll close my eyes and by the time I open them again it will have gone away.' If they study the cards for a few moments before closing their eyes they may have a strong hand – especially if the eye-closer is a woman. (Women are more likely to close our eyes at moments of ecstasy.)

Bluffing: In an experienced player this gesture must be a bluff. No one who is used to playing the game would need to reel away from a hand in this way. They're miming thinking or reflecting – which means they probably don't need to.

DRAMATIC GESTURES

Dramatic gestures are used either by a complete novice who just wants to show off, or a player who is new to bluffing and hasn't got the message that less is more. If the former, be happy for them and try not to fleece them too much – especially if it's your mother. If the latter, pretend to believe them while assuming that whatever gestures they make, the opposite is true.

INDECISION

Rocking or nodding

A whole-body rocking motion is an extreme self-comfort gesture commonly used by small children. A more subtle rocking of the body, from side to side or back and forth, is a sign of indecision. It's as though we are trying to give our body a shake to get the thought processes going. Sometimes this gesture may involve a slight sideways movement of the head alone.

Bluffing: An experienced player is unlikely to use this gesture as a bluff as it's easily translated in many different ways. Most bluffers will employ more linear gestures that are unlikely to be misunderstood. Don't confuse this with a nodding head movement, which could indicate that players are trying to drive the game on. This is a much more urgent movement – a sign of building excitement suggesting players believe they're on the brink of a win.

Eyes darting back and forth

This eye movement is like someone searching in cupboards for something they've lost and is another sign of indecision. By switching from recalled memory to imagination they're showing they don't even know which cupboard to look in!

Bluffing: This would be a very unusual bluff as the gesture itself would spark a feeling of indecision. It's also very difficult to perform consciously.

Eyes darting between cards in hand

Now this is probably quite common just after the cards have been dealt as players estimate their hands and I'd avoid reading too much into it. If it continues for too long, though, they're acting in an indecisive way.

Bluffing: This is unlikely to be a bluff because most fake eye-movements are hard to do. Exceptions are the less subtle ones such as a long hard stare or averted gaze.

Hand-wringing

The hand-wring is an obvious gesture of both indecision and anxiety. The hands are common indicators of non-verbal leakage and so while the hand-wring sounds theatrical it happens more often than you might think. The gesture is partly self-comfort and partly obsessive. Don't confuse it with the rapid hand-rub which is a gesture of eager anticipation and normally performed as players sit down to play.

Bluffing: Hand-wringing could be used as a bluff although the obvious problem is that the hands have to be free. If experienced players put their cards down to hand-wring I would always smell a rat. They're performing an anxiety gesture so – as usual – suspect the opposite and assume they're confident about their hand.

NERVOUSNESS

Throat clearing or coughing

When we suffer from performance nerves we often get what's called 'a frog in the throat'. Public speakers and presenters who forget to warm up beforehand may start off trying to clear their throat. The problem would never arise in normal conversation. If opponents are clearing their throat, listen to when it happens. If it's just before their turn to play it could be that they're nervous about speaking up in the room. It's a bit like a best man before the wedding speech. If it happens as they study their cards I'd suggest they're nervous about the play rather than the performance. Do they do it all the time, even when they're winning? Look for patterns of behaviour. The advantage of monitoring throat-clearing is that you don't have to look up to do it.

Bluffing: This is an easy bluff to use but it's not so easy to know when to use it. If a player is using throat-clearing as a bluff they'll probably perform it as they're 'thinking' about their cards or just before they place their bet, to suggest that 'I shouldn't really be doing this, I'm taking a big risk.'

Lightning smile

A genuine smile touches the eyes and spreads evenly across the face. It is slow to grow and stays in place for several seconds. A rapid or 'lightning' smile is more likely to indicate nervousness. This is social smiling gone into overdrive.

Bluffing: Lightning smiles are rarely adopted as a bluff. They feel false and so an experienced bluffer will pick a more natural bluff for fear of being caught out. If a bluffer flashes a lightning smile it's probably a bluff gone wrong. They're trying to smile their way through a bad hand to convince you it's a good one but the smile just won't hold in place.

Chattering

If players chatter by nature this could just be their normal behaviour. But if it increases during the game it will usually be prompted by what's happening. Beware of chatter that increases right at the end of the game, though. With an inexperienced player this could be the 'winning nerves' that we saw can cause shaking hands. Don't assume the chatterer is heading for disaster.

Bluffing: Nervous chatter is a hard bluff to perform – you'd need to be a top-class actor. I would suggest only a really experienced player might try it. It involves too many elements (thinking, body language and speaking) to be first choice for a clever bluff.

Head rolling

These are Mike Tyson-style head-rolls that boxers employ to relax the neck muscles and intimidate their opponents in the ring. The head-roll has become a gesture of machismo although the basic purpose is to relieve anxiety.

Bluffing: This is a difficult bluff to pull off because of its two potential meanings: nervousness or strength. Is the bluffer pretending to be suffering from anxiety or trying to look like a tough guy?

ANALYSIS OF YOUR OPPONENTS' BODY GESTURES

Nail-worrying

Nail-biting is such an obvious sign of nervousness that it is almost bound to be genuine. Would any bluffer worth their salt really employ such an old cliché? However, there are subtler variants, such as nail-picking, rubbing or playing with or chewing at hangnails. These are common gestures of anxiety and might continue throughout the game. If constant you can assume opponents are tense but you'll need to study their behaviour for accelerations at key moments to spot the clues about their hand.

Bluffing: If experienced players nail-bite you can assume they're traditionalists as far as bluffs are concerned. This is such an obvious ploy it could be a double-bluff.

Sweating

Assuming this is not due to the temperature, or physical causes, sweating is usually read as nervousness. Because it involves an unconscious physiological mechanism, it can't really be performed as a bluff. So, what exactly does sweating tell us? Before you assume nervousness, ask yourself whether the room is too warm or the player overweight. Check for shiny faces or damp sweat patches before the game starts to see if sweatiness is the norm. A middle-aged woman might be suffering a hot flush. People who suddenly sweat don't usually have any way of coping with it. A sweaty type will normally whip out a hankie or employ well-used ways of dealing with the flow. Sweating under pressure should normally be assumed to be anxiety-caused. The sweater will often dab or wipe nervously and appear embarrassed. As with shaking hands or nervous laughter or chatter, though, it might indicate excitement over a good hand as much as anxiety over a poor one.

Silence

Silence is the verbal equivalent of poker face – closing down body language signals when you want to lie, unless the player is also quiet in normal life. Sudden silences can suggest periods of intense concentration. This alone should give clues about the player's hand. Why would they need to think hard if the hand is good? Are they assessing their chances of getting away with a bluff?

MICRO-GESTURES

These fleeting expressions are like subliminal messages: so speedy as to be virtually invisible to the naked eye, they can nevertheless be detected once you become sensitive to them. Micro-gestures are often confined to the face, which makes them rich pickings for the poker player. They are also very valuable because they are key leakages that we perform. They're virtually impossible to do consciously and convincingly and the information they reveal is dramatic.

If you monitor a player's face carefully it is often possible to spot one fleeting expression that may be completely at odds with the masked or performed one. If you catch it you could be onto a winner. Here's how to assess the information – ask yourself:

- What did the micro-gesture look like? Anger? Fear? Disgust? Revulsion? Agony? Ecstasy?
- What would an expression like that tell you under normal circumstances, if it was prolonged?
- Was this fleeting expression at odds with their normal or performed look?

ANALYSIS OF YOUR OPPONENTS' BODY GESTURES

When filmed and examined in slow motion, these micro-gestures seem pleasingly exaggerated. It's as though the effort of covering up our true feelings produces an explosion of expression that gives the game away. Perhaps these gestures were originally nature's way of ensuring that we couldn't be fooled. The problem is we are no longer as sensitive or perceptive as we used to be. Once we tune into these micro-gestures, however, they can be laughably revealing.

Spotting the micro

It's useful to have a spotter's guide to our most obvious and instinctive facial expressions, so that we can recognise them when they appear as micro-gestures. The eyes and especially the eyebrows are perhaps the most 'honest' communicators on the face. Pay special attention to this area when looking for micro-gestures.

Disgust
- Wrinkled nose.
- Eyes closed.
- Looking away.
- Eyes squeezed shut.
- Facial wince: eyes closed, mouth shut and puckered.
- Tongue tip poking though front of lips.

Dislike
- Gritting of teeth.
- Curled top lip.
- Eyes raised.
- Eyes rolled to ceiling in arc.

Fear
- Eyes widened.
- Eyebrows raised and pulled together.
- Tense lower eyelid, raised upper eyelid.
- Hand clamped over mouth.
- Face drawn back.

Sadness
- Corners of mouth pulled downwards.
- Eyes dropping downwards.
- Inner corner of the eyebrow pulled upwards.
- Frown in middle of eyebrows.
- Mouth puckered in middle.

Surprise
- Raised eyebrows.
- Widened eyes.
- Mouth puckered into a round, whistling shape.

Celebration
- Hand clenched into raised fist.
- Sides of mouth stretched out horizontally, teeth edge-to-edge.

Happiness, enjoyment
- Tongue licks at corner of mouth.

Indecision
- Eyes roll from one side to the other.
- Cheeks puff out.
- Lips purse.
- Mouth-shrug.

Anger at own hand
- Eyebrows knitted in middle.
- Mouth snarling.
- Lips closed and pulled tightly inwards.
- Bitten lower lip.
- Lips narrowed.

Anger at opponent's hand
- Head pushed forward.
- Stare.
- Lips narrowed.
- Lips pulled back to show teeth.
- Nostrils flared.

CULTURAL DIFFERENCES

If you play with people of different cultures you will notice differences in what are deemed to be appropriate and inappropriate levels of emotional display, and this can affect the way you read your opponents. For example, Japanese culture discourages displays of high levels of emotion. British culture can be similar in some aspects – we are famous for keeping a 'stiff upper lip'. However there are six basic emotions that are identifiable via facial expressions in nearly all cultures:

- Happiness.
- Sadness.
- Anger.
- Surprise.
- Fear.
- Disgust/contempt.

DOUBLE BLUFFS

As if the straightforward bluff isn't complex enough, true actors will be looking to advance their skills into the double bluff. This is usually produced after a session of alternating bluffing and non-bluffing when players need a new angle to confuse their opponents. This is how it works.

Your opponents study their hand. Let's say it's a weak one. They then:

- Suppress their disappointment/annoyance signals.
- Imagine the single bluff, that is performing the reverse, which would be pleasure or anticipation.
- Suppress the desire to perform this single bluff.
- Perform the first response instead, that is act out disappointment/annoyance.

Often this is a very 'savant' bluff performance. By this stage in the game you will be aware that this player is bluffing. They may have even unveiled several single bluffs already. You know they're bluffing but is it a single or double bluff? At this point your brain could well be spinning in confusion. You may wish you'd stuck to Snap.

Sometimes the bluffer might even be arrogant enough to smile, coming out of costume for a moment to confuse you more. The only hope you have by this stage is if you studied their response when they first looked at their cards and there was a flicker of something genuine there. Otherwise play according to logic and statistics. Know when to quit.

15

SLEDGING

Until the 2006 World Cup, most people thought 'sledging' was an event at the Winter Olympics. Cricket players muttered darkly about it and we saw early examples on the build-up to big boxing matches but it hadn't really reached the psyche of the great British public. Now, thanks to the astonishing behaviour of Messrs Wayne Rooney and Zinedine Zidane, it's the latest technique for winning world-class games.

So what is sledging? This is the trick of making pointed or wounding remarks in order to get your opponents wound up and so put them off their game. The more wounding the remarks the better. This is no simple 'Jug ears!' name calling. To be an expert sledger you need to know exactly what comments will cause maximum fall-out.

It worked in the World Cup where Rooney and Zidane were sent off for aggressive behaviour triggered by getting a roasting from a member of the opposing team. Nobody knows for sure exactly what was said to them but the result was a complete loss of cool resulting in acts of violence and ending in red cards. If professional football players can be wound up in this way, poker players will be just as susceptible.

Now I don't propose that you spit at your poker opponents or doubt their parentage. But it is possible to wind someone up using simple and often subtle body language gestures. This technique is called 'non-verbal sledging' or 'red rag bodytalk' and it can be accidental, unintentional or blatant gamesmanship. So here is a guide to the best-used tactics aimed at putting you off your stride. If you use them on others be prepared for a violent reaction. If they are directed at you, whatever you do, don't lose your temper.

Staring

Hard staring can be guaranteed to give you the willies. When an opponent stares hard it implies he or she is watching you closely because you're about to lose big-time. It's done to unnerve you, which is why you mustn't let it. It's gamesmanship of the corniest and most obvious kind.

Smirking

Totally childish, this is done with the intention of making you seem inferior, as in 'He's smirking so he must know something I don't which must mean he's a better player and knows he can beat me. He's telling me I'm rubbish.'

Ignoring

By looking away as you make your deliberations or place your bet your opponents are trying to imply that you are of no consequence, that they have the hand of all hands and that you cannot stand in the way of their success. As if!

SLEDGING

Pit-baring
When an opponent bares their armpits at you it's the most basic of put-downs in the animal kingdom. When we respect an opponent we keep our body and cards defended and protected. By sticking their hands behind their head and baring vulnerable body parts your opponents are trying to let you know they do not feel threatened by you.

The false smile
A genuine smile has an important social function, showing you mean no harm to the person it's aimed at. A false, stretched smile is completely the opposite. This is teeth-baring and in the animal kingdom it signals a desire to attack.

Pouting
What might normally be an expression of attraction becomes an insult when it's used around the poker table. Aiming a pout at someone means you find them childish and their game is immature. It signals you think they're sulking or you feel sorry for them.

Folded arms
When opponents fold their arms in your direction it suggests they've switched off and have no further interest in you. It implies they know they can beat you with one hand tied behind their back.

Eye-rolling

This is a completely hateful put-down. The eye-roll suggests the gesture's victim is completely useless and tiresome and a waste of space to boot.

According to poker player Simon Freedman, if sledging occurs it's usually done subtly: '*I actually try to draw it out against me,*' he says. '*This can make them feel I'm having a bad night and then they feel sorry for me. This way you play the player, giving them a false confidence.*'

16

PLAYING ONLINE

Margot O'Donoghue is a psychoanalyst who describes herself as a poker fan. Although she mostly plays online, she recently played in Las Vegas with 'real people'. Because her online play is 'invisible' what would normally be described as her 'tells' are free-spirited enough to be complete give-aways at an actual poker table: *'When I play at home on the Internet I'm childishly waving my arms in the air and expressing myself.'* It's interesting to note that these bad habits created a strong urge to take the opposite approach in her real game and adopt a static form of poker face. *'When I played in Vegas my daughter said we all looked so miserable at my table.'*

Maybe you don't think you'll be seduced onto the tables for fun or profit. Don't be so sure. Wait until you get bored with online and want to move on to the next 'fix' of adrenaline. Wait until you start to develop your game and want to pit your wits against the big boys. Wait until you want that added dimension of seeing your opponents break down as you relieve them of their car, house and plasma TV.

Okay, so perhaps one of the joys of playing online is that you can simultaneously bluff or bet while laughing like a demon at the good hand you've got or showing off to the neighbours who you have invited in for a drink. In many ways online poker is body language 'safe'. However, keep in mind the following:

Many online players, like Margot, switch to playing at real tables, face-to-face. Virtual reality becomes real life. If you've been muttering to yourself, laughing out loud, punching the air or strumming the banjo while playing online it will be very hard to break the habit when your opponents can actually see you. In many ways it will have become part of your thought processes. It will feel odd to play without doing it. You may even develop some or all of these 'tics' without realising it.

Now, depending on how long you've been playing in this manner, this could be a very hard habit to break. Do you really want added pressure when you're playing mean-looking dudes around the table? Of course you don't. Won't it be hard enough working out what you want to do to perform a bluff, or keeping your poker face in place, without also trying to eliminate a habit you didn't even know you'd developed until the cards were being dealt?

So rule number one in online poker is:

Play online as though playing face-to-face.

Another point to keep in mind: there is a strong element of psychology in online poker too, even though you can't be seen. You must still try to glean clues about your opponents and their behaviour. You will still need to work out how they bet and what type of game they tend to play. And there are several ways of doing this.

Of course you can always play like a robot or a buffoon. The joy of buffoon-poker is no-one gets to snigger at you face-to-face. Your stupidity will be anonymous. Which is why it's a good way to learn how to play and to experiment without much embarrassment.

In the world of online poker there is a term called 'slot players'. These are players who bet and raise the largest amounts they can on each game. They are being compared to people who use slot machines. They would lose money in a cash game but when it's just tokens involved they have enough success to keep using this tactic. This will create bad betting habits, though, so rule number two in online poker is:

Play as though you were playing face-to-face.

Yes, I know this is the same as rule number one, but this time I'm referring to your betting psychology. Never play as though you were just trading tokens. Again, you might think you have no intention of ever playing for money, and a big pat on the back for you if you stick to that, but . . . should you ever make the transition because you seem to be successful on the token front, you'll very likely lose your entire stash of cash unless you're very careful. Why? Because you've learned bad habits again.

A radio station once put together a team to gamble on the stock market, but without using actual money. They just kept a tab of imaginary cash. At the end of a year they'd made a healthy 'profit' and quite reasonably judged that their techniques were good enough to inject some real cash. Of course, they lost the lot. When there's no element of risk we just don't play the same. Risks are less risky. High stakes are not so high. So always play as though it was your own money out there, even if it's just tokens on a screen or peanuts on a table.

ONLINE PERSONALITY

Whenever you play online you'll adopt a personality all of your own and others will be trying to read you. You might think there's not much room for movement on this one but you'd be wrong. Margot O'Donoghue has noticed a whole raft of ways to pick out a player's personality profile from their play:

'Online you get to know characters like the ego-trippers who will be very loose in their play and bluff more. I can even pick out nationality differences from styles of play and will often make notes about how much a player tends to bet. You can talk online too, using code. I disguise my gender and play as a male so I often get called M8 (mate).'

Margot even had to remember to maintain her gender mask when she saw sexual harassment going on: *'There were two women having a go at a Welsh guy during one game. He flirted with them and they rejected him and he got progressively ruder as the game went on. I was dying to get involved but had to remember my assumed gender role.'*

The chat box can give away too many clues about you, so as a general rule, try to avoid getting too chatty.

LONER POKER

Much of the popularity of the Internet stems from the fact that it is ideal for the lone user. Lonely people across the world use it as a substitute for real friends, real life and real love/sex. However, I would draw the line at using online poker as a way of finding company. Poker players – proper ones who are looking to win – don't do chat. Any comments you write will be seen by everyone.

This might sound like a good place to try a bluff. You could try to appear thick, or impulsive, or whatever style of personality you think might help your game, and yes, it might just work. But first, look at your winning strategy.

Do you want to create a persona for yourself? Does it sound too tempting to miss out on? If so, why? Is your logical brain in gear during this decision or your emotional one? Do you see the chance to bluff like this as being logically advantageous? Or does it just sound like a fun idea? Try it and see. Fun's good but fun isn't long-term profit or long-term winning. Fun is its own form of 'win' but it won't be teaching you how to play well. If that's your goal, stay out of the chat box.

Big chatters are normally bad players. Some players keep a running commentary of their own hands. You're not going to be one of them. Or they spar with their opponents. But why wind them up? This is testosterone-fuelled power-posturing to the point where they must be more into the fun of the teasing and abuse than they are winning the game. Otherwise they'd stop giving away so much information about themselves.

However, is there any gain in reading the chat box to get clues about your opponents? Well, first the up-side. If they're using it genuinely, that is, in a lonely-hearts-let's-be-virtual-friends kind of way, you'll immediately be aware that they are:

- Lonely, and
- Not really there for the poker.

Also they could be sociopaths.

True online game-players can be divided into two categories:

- The ones who just want to power-posture and are hoping they can egg you into making a mistake by a series of dares and insults.
- The players who are adopting a persona with a view to creating a bluff.

The ones trying to psych you out are obviously very juvenile and possibly playing at home, in their parents' house, with a pretend Stetson on their head. The ones trying to bluff are possibly not being very subtle. They could well have adopted a different gender. (Some men pretend to be women, thinking that other players will then underestimate their abilities, and both men and women may pretend to be cool, older and more experienced players in an attempt to intimidate.)

Please keep in mind that the chat box is a bit like e-mail, only harder. Think how hard it is to read anyone via e-mail. You have a 99.9 per cent chance of misreading the emotional content of a sent message. Much of your interpretation will be based on your own emotional state. I once got a call from a colleague who asked me what I thought about an e-mail he'd received from his new chief executive. It read 'Thanks a lot for all your hard work.' I said I thought he was thanking him. He said he thought he was being sarcastic. The chief executive then left on a two-week cruise, safe in the knowledge that his employee would have received and understood his last missive. In fact, he'd set in motion a chain of events that nearly led to his colleague quitting, owing to the paranoia that built up during the fortnight he was away.

At least with e-mail you've probably met/worked with the sender. With the chat box you don't know the other person from Adam. So, go easy on sending and receiving 'bluff' messages in the chat box. Online poker gives you the supreme opportunity to achieve a poker face with the minimum of effort. Why unmask yourself when there's no need? Only if you play purely and utterly for fun, that's why.

PLAYING OUT OF TURN

Does your opponent post or play out of position? If so it's an easy guess that he/she is not going to be a strong or experienced player, unless it's a performed bluff. Good players tend to be patient and only play when they have the 'button' (their turn to deal) or when it's a compulsory bet.

BETTING

The other facility in online poker is the online poker room 'lobby'. This has a column that tells you the average pot of each table. It's easy to read this in a linear way and head for the one that suits your preferred style of risk-taking. But hold hard before you head for a 'high' table in the hope of winning more tokens. This average pot tells you what the average pot win is on each table. If it looks high it could just be that someone's doing risky betting, gambling high on weaker hands.

TIMING

In many ways timing is the online equivalent of body language. If you're looking for psychological clues in a game that isn't face-to-face then the time players take to make a move could well give you some useful clues about the state of their hand. Long pauses that end in a check will suggest a weak hand but long pauses that end in a bet will often signal strength. Even this could be a bluff though, so study patterns and look for discrepancies even online.

Slow players who always take long pauses or who take them over obviously weak hands are often distracted their end. Because the players aren't visible it's up to them how seriously they want to play and if they want to watch TV or chat with friends at the same time. By judging the pauses and relating them to the hands you should be able to tell whether your opponent is suffering from attention deficit disorder or not.

The bet/raise or check/fold button that puts you on 'hold' can also be helpful in signalling your opponents' hands or style of play.

TAKE BREAKS

There's something about the Internet that makes people want to skip taking breaks. It's the same in the office and it's the same with computer games or chat rooms. Hours go by without anyone noticing. When you play poker online it's essential to take breaks. If you don't, you will suffer mental fatigue and that can lead to mistakes through poor concentration or memory lapses. So sit out some games once in a while, especially if you're losing badly or winning well. Get things into context and give your brain a rest. Spend the time thinking of nothing or daydreaming. This is like re-booting your brain and you'll play all the better for it.

DON'T DRINK

Poker and alcohol aren't the natural bedfellows they seem to be in cowboy movies. Beware of coming home late after a drunken evening out and logging on for a game before you hit the sack. This is every bit as dangerous as texting an ex-lover when you're inebriated. In the morning you'll regret it, I promise. Place a cover over the PC before you go out or hide the plug.

One final word of warning about under- or over-estimating your opponent online.

When Margot O'Donoghue was playing one evening she missed the start of one game so switched and joined another. When the cards came down she realised she was into a game she'd never played before . . .

'I thought I might as well stay in as I had chips by then so I had to Google the instructions for that game and I was reading them while I was playing. I didn't really care how I played as I didn't know what I should be doing and I just played like a lunatic. People started dropping out because they were scared of me as they had no idea what I was doing. I took on 45 players who knew how to play and ended up winning.'

IN SHORT . . .

So, to end, two key rules to guide you through the maze that is poker psychology, both online and at the table:

1. Never, ever underestimate the skill involved in making a good bluff or poker face.
2. Play for fun or play to win – either way your body language skills will enhance your game.

INDEX

INDEX

INDEX

INDEX